75 AUTHENTIC AND INSPIRED RECIPES

TACOS

MARK MILLER

WITH BENJAMIN HARGETT AND JANE HORN

PHOTOGRAPHY BY ED ANDERSON

TEN SPEED PRESS
Berkeley

CONTENTS

THE ART OF THE TACO

I had a New England childhood and was always interested in food, cooking, and particularly markets. They were and still are an adventure for me. I loved to go shopping with my mother at our local First National, which still had sawdust on the floor in front of the butcher department. Then there was the exotic Italian grocery with its massive, overflowing window displays of every product from their sun-drenched culture (so anti-Puritan in New England!), the stores for salami and sausages, the Jewish delis for pickles and lox, and the fishmongers for live lobsters with huge claws that crawled along the bottoms of the deep cold-water tanks.

I spent summers far away from New England in a more exotic culinary culture, in Mexico at a large hacienda near Guadalajara owned by family friends. In charge of the kitchen were three generations of cooks from one family—grandmother, mother, and daughter—whose food and sauces were sublime, a revelation to me. In the early mornings they would go to the market to buy the fresh masa for the day, the sweetest, most colorful fruits, the ripest fresh vegetables picked just hours earlier from local gardens, cuts of meat butchered from whole animals. I'd always tag along on this food adventure.

When the day's shopping was finished, we always had time for a taco—the street snack everyone eats when they're not at home or when they don't have the time or money to sit down at a restaurant. The women were as picky about tacos as they were about the ingredients for the daily meals. I would see all of the taco stands at the marketplace lined up. But my local "taco guides" were almost fierce in their determination

that we would eat only from their favorites. "This is the best for pork," they'd say, urging me to a particular stall. I would soon have a wonderful taco of carnitas in my hand—succulent browned pork pieces with a touch of green cilantro and spicy roasted tomatillo-árbol sauce, all wrapped with a fresh corn tortilla. It was so different from the bologna on soft white bread that I was used to back at school. This food was alive, colorful, aromatic, tasty, crunchy, juicy, flavorful—as if I had crossed a new frontier of food experience.

The tacos were always simple things—delicious aromatic stewed or grilled meat, a few leaves of cilantro, a bit of chopped white onion, a modest spoonful of spicy salsa, the freshly griddled tortilla lightly coated with cooking juices and tasting intensely of roasted corn. Cupping the taco in my hand, I sensed the warmth of the tortilla pulled seconds ago from a hot comal. It was a snack prepared as I watched, made as fresh as could be with ingredients often purchased just moments before at the same market. And everyone around me—adults, children, workers, tourists, business people—was buying, eating, and enjoying a taco just as I was, and then getting on with their day. When the market was over, the food eaten, the customers back home, at school, at work, the vendors closed up.

Street food as I knew it in the United States was never prepared on the spot. Vendors didn't cook, they assembled. Hot dogs and buns came from the factory and were kept warm in steamers, relish was portioned from a jar. Ice cream was scooped from tubs in a freezer or sold already packaged. Nothing was cooked from scratch in front of me. The tacos at the market were fast food unlike any I'd ever had in Boston.

There are taco trucks in parts of Boston today, as there are in any major American city with a large Hispanic population. But I never saw any growing up, certainly not on Cape Cod or in Maine, where we spent short holidays. But times have changed, and the taco has become an accepted part of American food culture. As a matter of fact, my good friend (and great chef) Ken Oringer opened a taqueria across from Fenway Park not long ago.

My market tacos were always finished in a few drippy mouthfuls. I loved how good they tasted, but just as much I loved the whole taco experience—it was fun, immediate, social, a constantly changing community of fellow taco eaters. No matter that some of us might also patronize expensive restaurants or had a cook at home. Or that others barely got by day to day. For one moment, in one place, we gathered round to eat something that costs almost nothing, sharing the setting, the culture, and the tastes of that particular place. Even today, part of what I love about eating tacos in Mexico is that it's still a shared cultural and aesthetic experience, an agreement on what good food is and, in particular, what good tacos are all about.

As I've traveled through Mexico in all the years that followed, I've learned which of the taco stands to head for in any particular place, the ones that tell me where I am and where I can eat good local cuisine better than any guidebook. It's that special sense of place that comes with eating local food in a particular environment, a comfortable "grounding" of where I am.

When I think about the Yucatán, and in particular its capital, Mérida, it's going to be the pork taco stand at the market, where you must go early, no later than 8 AM, or they will sell out of their specialty, the fantastic *cochinita pibil*—marinated suckling pig cooked overnight in a pit, served with an escabeche of red onions flavored with oregano and a little fiery habanero salsa. There is no other place that makes it like that one, where I've gone for thirty years. I wrap it all up in a warm corn tortilla and know that I'm now in Mérida.

In Ensenada, it's the vendor who comes in from the countryside only between 8 and 10 in the morning and sets up outside the lumber yard. He sells thirteen wonderful kinds of tacos from his flatbed truck, slow-cooked with meat from his own herds of goats and sheep. And all the local carpenters, construction workers, and passersby like me show up to buy and to eat them together.

In Guadalajara, it's the stand in a hard-to-find, way-out neighborhood open only from 7 to 10 in the evening, which prepares a very special taco made from cow's udder—*taco de ubre*. When I'm in Mexico City, it's the one just off the Zocalo that makes fish tacos cooked *a la plancha* (on a griddle), served with this wonderful *salsa brujo* (witch's salsa).

Tacos are as much a part of daily social life in Mexico as the Catholic Church. In all parts of Mexico, taco carts—*puestos*—spring up on every block, are crammed onto sidewalks, dot the plazas, litter the roadsides. In every little town or *pueblito* inevitably there will be a house or two with a taco truck as a semi-permanent fixture in the yard. The trucks may not have moved in years, but in the evenings they come alive to serve up Mexico's most popular snack food to the people of the town.

I can picture the taco stands being rolled into place in the evenings—a custom practiced all across Mexico. Fires are lit and counters wiped. Smoke rises lazily in small, crackling plumes, and the pungent aroma of chiles roasting over open flames permeates the air. Most of Mexico lies within the tropics. As the heat of the day fades, the streets fill up with people of all ages who stroll and mingle. Kids rush outdoors for pick-up soccer games. Food vendors, performers, and traveling sidewalk hawkers crowd downtown plazas as people come together outside. Park benches that were mostly empty throughout the day are now at a premium. Cars with huge speakers strapped to their roofs circle through the city blaring advertisements. Church doors open in preparation for evening visitors. Lines form at taco stands, attracting both workers on their way home and older people stepping out for an evening stroll. Throughout the evening, taco sellers remain busy as partygoers take to the streets. In many places, lines may be the longest during the earliest morning hours near the markets, bus and metro stops, the large office building complexes, or universities.

As with all street food sites, taco stands are ephemeral by nature (or, as we would call it today, exhibiting "just-in-time logistics"). They set up in a spot convenient to their customers, open when demand is high, close when it fades. Some taco vendors operate only for breakfast at the market, others appear just at midday in the plaza to catch workers on their lunch break. In the smaller towns, Sundays are an especially good day for tacos, particularly after church, when the congregation mixes socially to reaffirm its connections to its religion and its food customs. Specialty tacos are often prepared by locally renowned cooks on weekends as a sort of community service. They may have other jobs during the week, but love to practice their specialties and keep alive the regional culinary culture, not to mention earn a little extra money and catch up on the local gossip.

I want to excite people about tacos, the street food that gets my juices going every day that I'm in Mexico. I want the recipes in this book to get the point across that tacos aren't some strange, exotic fare. They are fun, immediate, inexpensive, healthy, modern—small portions that you can enjoy throughout the day. They're food that's fresh, fast, economical, and easy, a good match to the rapid pace of our modern lifestyle. The sauces and salsas are rich in vegetables and seasonings. Protein—meat, seafood, poultry—is an accessory, enjoyed in smaller amounts, as in Asian cuisines. You don't need lots of expensive equipment to make them. The techniques are simple. No years of culinary experience required (but a few years of eating tasty food help).

Use these recipes to see how much fun making and eating tacos can be. You'll find traditional favorites like Tacos al Pastor (page 76) and Baja-Style Tempura Fish Tacos (page 68) and my own taco innovations, from Thai Shrimp (page 59) to Chicken with Apples and Goat Cheese (page 46). Once you have an idea of what tacos are all about, start playing with the simple ingredients you have around. You can make a salsa out of just about anything in your refrigerator. You can create a taco from leftovers as quickly as you can throw together a sandwich made with grilled cheese, bologna, or peanut butter and jelly. And I think tacos are more fun, interesting, and healthy than any of these.

TACO BASICS

A taco can be any filling wrapped in a tortilla (the word *taco* comes from the Nahuatl word *ac,* meaning flat, which is what the Aztecs called this food form when the Spanish arrived). But tacos aren't just a basic preparation—take a tortilla and fill it. I see them as a way of personalizing our food, individualizing a culinary experience. You aren't simply ordering. You are building a meal in a totally hands-on way— choosing the filling, the garnishes, the salsas, the sauces, and how much of any of them you want. You can't really do that most of the time. Every time you have a taco, you have the opportunity for a unique culinary experience.

Tacos are quick to prepare because they are modular. You "build" a taco from its elements—the tortilla, the filling, the garnish, the salsa. I remember in particular one *taquero*—as the great Mexican taco masters are called—who could assemble a taco in three or four seconds. He had the tortillas and meat ready— pork, tripe, brisket—which he constantly moved around on the heat. With each order, the meat went into the tortilla, and he actually threw the onion and the cilantro garnish with one hand to the taco he was holding in the other. Done!

So think like a *taquero*. If you have the taco elements prepped and at hand, you're seconds away from serving (or eating) one. Get to know the fillings and side dishes in this book, but don't feel compelled to make everything from scratch. Even at the market-places in Mexico, a vendor who sells tacos with mole doesn't always make the mole herself. She'll go to the woman at the market who makes mole and buy it

from her. Then, she's on to the chicken lady for a bird. Returning to her little stand, she cooks the chicken and the mole and makes her tacos.

Experiment with prepared ingredients. Cooked "food to go" that only requires reheating at home is an exploding category at many upscale markets. Butcher shops have more interesting meats. I've counted seventeen different kinds of fresh sausage made in store at the meat counter of my local Whole Foods. If you buy links that are seasoned, just grill them, crumble them up, and you've got your taco filling. For salsas and sauces, there's a lot of help out there in the form of good ones that are already prepared. Frontera and Melinda's are some of my favorite brands.

Those of us who live in the Southwest can shop locally for most of the regional ingredients needed to prepare the recipes in this book. Otherwise, you'll have to do a little homework before you start cooking. See what's available in your area, either at the markets you visit often or at ones you've always wanted to get to know. You're likely to find almost everything you need within a reasonable distance of where you live if your city includes a large Hispanic population. Check out the web sites of the retailers listed in Sources (page 167). I've found the Hispanic search site www.comida.com an excellent resource for information about Hispanic foods, as is www.restmex.com, the web site of *El Restaurante Mexicano*, a magazine for the Latin foods industry. Community-backed sites like www.chowhound.com offer tips for travelers and locals alike about where to find the best tacos or ingredients for making them.

★ ★ ★

HEAT LEVELS

All the recipes in this book (where appropriate) are numbered according to a subjective heat reference, 10 being the hottest and 0 being the mildest. As 60 percent of the heat in a chile is in its ribs or veins, with 30 percent in the seeds and 10 percent in the flesh, you can moderate the fire of any dish by removing the ribs, veins, and seeds of a chile, or the seeds alone.

★ ★ ★

TACO FILLINGS

Recipes for taco fillings make up most of the chapters, with the salsas and side dishes each having a chapter of their own. All the fillings have suggestions for tortillas and accompaniments, as well as beverages. The basics of tortillas follow in the section "About Tortillas" (page 10).

Tacos are like edible artifacts of Mexican history, culture, and geography as well as a platform for your own creativity. The fillings in this book deliciously demonstrate this variety. Pork Carnitas (page 78) and Chicken with Mole Verde from Puebla (page 40) offer traditional and regional tastes. Calamari with Blackened Tomato (page 60) reflects coastal abundance. Tacos al Pastor (page 76) have Mediterranean roots. You'll also find tacos that are personal riffs inspired by the flavors I grew up with, re-creations of taste memories from my travels, and spins on regional American classics, although they all connect in some way to the Mexican kitchen. Lobster and Avocado (page 64) reprises an extravagant lunch I had in the English countryside, but I've tasted similar pairings in Mexico. Chicken with Rajas and Corn (page 45) combines sweet summer corn with barbecued chicken, flavors born in the American South. I encourage you to try the flavors you love in taco form.

★ ★ ★

SALSAS AND SIDES

You'll find recipes in the chapter "Sides and Drinks" for classic taco accompaniments like rice flavored with chiles and herbs, smoky cowboy beans, and those staples of Mexican platters everywhere—*refritos*, refried beans, cooked two ways, as well as my favorite guacamole. I've also included several slaws that will add a pleasant vegetable crunch to your tacos as well as some protection to crispy tortillas from sauces that could make them soggy. In the chapter "Salsas" you'll enjoy getting to know about ten different salsas and sauces that will brighten your tacos with just a small spoonful.

At its simplest, a salsa is a condiment whose flavorful ingredients are raw, partially raw, or cooked, and that are combined together but never cooked together (in a sauce, the ingredients *are* cooked together). A well-conceived salsa should have layers of flavors that stay unique and separate in your mouth. No single ingredient should take over: you want to taste each one—the sweetness of the tropical fruit, the sharp bite of onion, the aromatic herbal essence of cilantro, the lively heat of the chile.

Any taco stand will offer salsa fresca—a simple mix of chopped fresh tomatoes, diced onions, cilantro leaves, minced chiles, and lime. Vendors make it on the spot and only in small amounts—part of the logistics of the stand itself as they don't make anything they can't prepare on a small cutting board. It tastes best when eaten within an hour or two of preparation, another reason why it's not made in quantity. If a stand runs out—they're at a market, after all—they buy more tomatoes, cilantro, and onions from a nearby stall. If you can't make your own salsa fresca, buy one at a store that sells it the same day that it's made. Salsa frescas that sit on a supermarket refrigerator shelf for two or three days aren't worth eating.

Garnishes and salsas at a Mexican taco cart are limited to a classic few, plus occasionally something regional. Don't expect a salsa bar with dozens of choices, and don't feel the need to set one up at home. Most typical are salsa fresca, fresh or roasted tomatillo salsa (salsa verde), cooked salsa rojo (a red salsa with dried red chile as the base), chopped fresh cilantro, chopped onion, and pickled jalapeños. Chile salsas tend to reflect their location: a salsa from the Yucatán will include the fiery habanero chile; one from coastal Veracruz will always include fresh tropical fruit.

Here are my Basic Seven for a salsa bar: one raw (that is, fresh, like Salsa Fresca, page 130), one cooked (such as Tomatillo–Árbol Chile Salsa, page 135), something pickled (try Pickled Onions with Sweet Bell Peppers, page 146), plus Mexican crema (or crème fraîche) or sour cream, chopped cilantro, chopped white onion, and lime wedges.

One final tip—use salsa in moderation. Mexicans understand that salsa is an accent, unlike Americans, who tend to have this bravado about loading up their tacos with the hottest salsa on the table. Too much salsa can completely ruin the taste of a dish. It would be like burying the pastrami on your sandwich beneath six kinds of pickles plus tomatoes, onions, sauerkraut, and cheese. What happened to the meat? Minimize too-much-salsa syndrome at your table: dole out salsas with the smallest spoon in your drawer, if necessary.

★ ★ ★

BUILDING A TACO

Building a taco is a quick process. If you can do as much of the preparation as possible in advance, you can have everything ready and waiting for your hungry guests. Most of the fillings—which typically are either quickly cooked or require long slow cooking—can be made ahead and hold well. Or you can buy the time-intensive ingredients ready made, for example, in the form of rotisserie chicken or pulled pork. Vegetables like chiles, tomatoes, corn, and garlic that require roasting are also perfect candidates for advance preparation. Otherwise, prepare what you need in reverse order: make the salsas first, as they need to marry for an hour or so. Chop the fresh garnishes—cilantro, onion, fennel—and arrange in little serving dishes. Let the meat, chicken, or fish marinate, then cook the filling quickly just before serving. Tortillas can be made ahead by you or purchased and warmed at the last minute.

The goal when building a taco is to create distinct layers of flavor, from the tortilla on up. Handmade tortillas have an inside and an outside (something like the grain of meat or even paper), which determines how easily they fold. The outside (the "bottom") of a handmade tortilla will be thicker and browner as it is the side that was cooked first. The filling should always go on the inside (the "top") of a tortilla—the side that was cooked second. Hold the tortilla in your hand and see which way it cups naturally; the concave side is the inside—that side that should face up when you add the filling. Figuring out which side of the tortilla is the bottom and which is the top is not as crucial with store-bought tortillas because they are pressed so uniformly by machine that they fold well either way. Spoon on the filling, followed by the salsas (not too much) and garnishes. Enjoy your taco.

For tacos made in crispy shells, you might want the first layer to be something like a bean puree or shredded cabbage, which will keep the shell from getting soggy, as will cooking the filling a little drier. On the other hand, when building a soft taco, you want the filling to be moist and saucy, which helps round out the corn flavor of the corn tortilla.

I've noticed at the Coyote Café how much people like to create their own food experience, adding more pork, more beans, more toppings to a dish so it's exactly as they like it. Tacos are a great party food for just that reason. You can assemble and serve a platter's worth of tacos at a time and let guests add their own finishing touches. Or let them build their own, one at a time, with fillings kept warm on the stove or on hot plates, tortillas held in containers or wrapped in a warm, damp cloth to keep them pliable, and garnishes and salsas available in serving bowls.

ABOUT TORTILLAS

In smaller towns and rural areas of Mexico where traditional cultural practices are respected and still followed, you can still hear the slap, slap of the tortilla maker—always a woman—coming from home kitchens, the market, or local restaurants and taco stands, as she pats fresh masa (a dough made from ground fermented dried corn) into flat disks ready for cooking on a hot comal.

In some ways, tortillas and their preparation have changed very little since before the arrival of the Spanish conquistadores in the 1500s. To make masa, dried corn kernels are boiled, then steeped in an alkaline solution of water and slaked lime (calcium hydroxide, or cal) to soften the kernels and loosen the hard outer hulls. The treated corn (*nixtamal*, in Spanish) is then washed to drain off the soaking solution and filter out the hulls, and ground with a stone roller on a flat grinding surface (*metate*) into a fine paste—the basis for masa.

In some ancient cultures, cal was mixed with ash, and the process became known as "nixtamalization" from the Nuhuatl (Aztec) words for "ash" and "corn dough." Nixtamalization also improves the nutritional value of corn by releasing some of the essential amino acids that are absorbed as nutrients. Without this processing, corn does not provide a balanced nutritional food. The Mesoamerican civilizations that followed this practice were protected from certain deficiency diseases like pellagra that plagued Europeans, who did not ferment their corn.

While we still appreciate handmade foods, including tortillas, tortilla preparation today is more and more a fully mechanized process—the masa is made and tortillas are pressed by machine. And tortillas are sold in most supermarket chains across the United States, so anyone with a yen to make tacos can find them. If you live in an area that has a regional marketplace, as I do in the Southwest, along with national brands like Mission, you'll also find commercially prepared tortillas made by local companies. Bueno Foods of Albuquerque, New Mexico, for example, makes an organic, stone-ground tortilla carried in area markets.

The best corn tortillas for tacos are found at *tortillerias*, shops that make their own masa and tortillas, or at large Mexican groceries with a section that sells handmade tortillas. Not only are these tortillas fresher, they'll also probably be a good buy. Check online or in the classified section of the phone book for Mexican markets and get to know what they offer. Fresh flour tortillas are harder to find outside the border states; sometimes Mexican bakeries make them from the flour used for pastries and bread.

Probably the most widely available choice in this country is packaged corn and flour tortillas from chain supermarkets, usually found stacked on shelves near the Hispanic foods. The refrigerated sections of markets might carry fresh, preservative-free corn tortillas that are locally made—a better choice, if you can find them. The freshest tortillas are those made that day and sold nonrefrigerated. Avoid frozen tortillas, as they dry out and are difficult to handle.

Taco-sized tortillas—about 5½ inches—can be hard to find at supermarkets, which typically carry larger sizes for burritos and wraps. If you're a regular customer at a Mexican restaurant, ask where they buy their tortillas or check out the source used by the taco trucks that spring up at lunchtime in many urban areas—it's certain to be nearby. If you do track down a tortilla shop, tell them the tortillas are for tacos, so you'll get the right size. If you can't find small tortillas, you can always cut down larger tortillas to the size you need.

Should you use yellow or white corn tortillas? There's no nutritional difference and very little flavor difference between them. To me, yellow corn is a little earthier, while white corn tends be a little sweeter and lighter in flavor. The choice of yellow or white corn tortillas is more personal preference—what tastes right to you with any particular filling.

What about flour tortillas? To most Mexicans, the idea of eating a taco wrapped in a flour tortilla is a totally foreign concept. You would never see flour tortillas at a Mexican taco stand. In fact, you won't see flour tortillas at all south of Mexico City (except perhaps at tourist resorts). They're more common regionally, in the northern states like Sonora and Sinaloa, or along the border with Texas as part of Tex-Mex cuisine. For the fillings in the book that have a Southwestern accent like Chicken with Apples and Goat Cheese (page 46), Elk Tenderloin with Green Chile Dry Rub (page 105), or Buffalo Sausage (page 106), flour tortillas are a good choice.

★ ★ ★

HOLDING AND REWARMING TORTILLAS
Part of the fun of eating a taco is building them assembly-line fashion, so you want the tortillas warm, soft, and ready to eat. You can cook fresh tortillas at home up to one hour ahead of serving and hold them wrapped in a damp cloth, in a bamboo steamer, or rice cooker—any setup that keeps the tortillas moist and warm, but not wet (as long as the tortilla stays warm, it stays flexible).

To ready all types of tortillas for serving—handmade or otherwise—heat them until they puff up a little or soften over an open flame (hold with tongs, or carefully, with your fingers) or on a dry heavy-bottomed, seasoned cast-iron skillet or griddle over high heat (a two-burner pancake griddle lets you warm a bunch of tortillas at a time). You want to gently heat them so they're flexible and develop that roasted corn taste, but not long enough that they cook. Don't heat corn or flour tortillas in a microwave, as they get hard. At the table, keep tortillas pliable by wrapping them in a damp cloth or stacking them in a tortilla "safe" (a covered container).

★ ★ ★

MAKING TORTILLAS
If you live in an area where there are no fresh tortillas available in the local grocery store, you can make them at home (although in my experience, buying tortillas in most areas of the United States doesn't seem to be a problem—anywhere you have a Spanish-speaking population, you will find tortillas).

For corn tortillas, start with fresh masa or with masa harina—ground dehydrated masa (masa harina is not cornmeal, but an entirely different product in flavor and performance). Fresh masa is carried at most Mexican markets or *tortillerias*; ask for masa *simple*

(SIM-play) for tortillas, not the prepared masa (masa *preparada*) usually used for tamales, as the texture of the latter won't work for tortillas as it is already mixed with shortening. Masa harina is sold at almost every Hispanic market and well-stocked chain supermarkets.

Preparing corn tortillas from scratch seems a simple process—form masa into a ball, flatten the dough between the plates of a tortilla press, and quickly cook the dough disk on a hot comal or griddle. Simple, yes, but early efforts may feel more frustrating than foolproof. Variables from the consistency of the masa to your technique with a tortilla press to the pan you cook on can affect the outcome. With familiarity—from practice—come success, new skills, and even

the chance to create new flavors for unique tacos with add-ins like herbs, spices, cocoa powder, or chile powders, a Mexican culinary tradition that dates to pre-Columbian times.

For equipment, you'll need a heavy-duty electric mixer with dough hook attachment for beating the masa (or a bowl and wooden spatula, if mixing by hand), a metal or wooden tortilla press (see page 166), and a flat cast-iron comal (see page 156) or griddle, preferably oblong or rectangular to fit over two burners so you can cook multiple tortillas at a time. Another good choice is a rectangular electric nonstick pancake griddle. I don't recommend a skillet, as its high sides get in the way.

CORN TORTILLAS

MAKES APPROXIMATELY 12 (5½-INCH) CORN TORTILLAS
OR 24 (4-INCH) MINI TORTILLAS

To make tortillas with masa harina, use packaged masa harina. Two of the most widely available brands are Maseca (be sure to buy the type for tortillas) and Quaker Oats. One of my favorites is an all-natural, stone-ground masa harina made by Bob's Red Mill, a small Oregon company that specializes in whole grain products. You can find it at Whole Foods markets, natural food stores, well-stocked specialty markets, supermarkets, and online. Purchase masa harina from a supermarket with a high turnover, as it will go rancid over time. Always taste masa harina before you use it to be sure it is still fresh. It does not store well and goes off much faster than flour. It's best to store masa harina in the refrigerator or freezer, where it holds for 2 to 3 months. It will also keep in your pantry if sealed airtight for about 2 months. Making the dough is easiest in a heavy-duty mixer, but you can also mix it by hand in a bowl with a wooden spatula.

2 cups Bob's Red Mill masa harina

1¼ cups plus 2 tablespoons warm water

¼ teaspoon fine kosher or table salt

★ ★ ★

To make the dough, in the bowl of a heavy duty electric mixer fitted with a dough hook, add the masa harina, the water, and salt. Beat at medium speed until all the water is incorporated and a smooth dough forms without any masa sticking to the sides of the bowl. It should be a little wet at this stage as it will continue to absorb water during the resting stage. Cover the masa dough with plastic wrap and let sit at room temperature until the masa is denser than bread dough, but moister than pasta dough, 30 to 60 minutes. You want the masa to absorb all the moisture from the water. If it's too dry, you'll find it difficult to form tortillas, which will be brittle and dry when cooked, rather than pliable and soft.

To work with the masa, hands must be moist, but not wet. Have a small bowl of warm water nearby. To form 5½-inch tortillas, divide the dough into 12 equal portions (about 1½ ounces each) and form them into 1½-inch balls. For mini 4-inch tortillas, divide the dough into 24 equal portions (about 1 ounce each) and form 1-inch balls. Keep the balls of masa covered with a damp towel until you cook them.

To prepare the tortilla press, first line it with plastic so the masa won't stick. Use a quart-size, heavy-duty (freezer-weight) plastic bag. Trim off the sides, but not the bottom, open the bag like a book, and center half the sheet of plastic on the bottom plate of the press, letting the other half drape down.

CONTINUED ▶

To press the tortillas, place 1 ball of masa slightly off center (away from the handle) between the plastic sheets on the bottom plate of the press, pressing down hard to flatten the dough into a thin, even circle. Drape the other half of the plastic bag over the masa. Close the press and apply firm, even pressure to flatten the dough to a 5½-inch tortilla (4-inch tortilla for mini) that's about ⅛ inch thick. With practice, you'll get to know how much pressure you'll need. Open the press and carefully peel off the top plastic. Flip the tortilla onto your hand and peel off the bottom sheet of plastic. Note: If the edges of the tortilla are cracked, the dough was too dry. Return the masa balls to the mixer bowl, beat in more water, and reform into balls.

To cook the tortillas, preheat a dry seasoned cast-iron comal or griddle over medium heat. Gently place the tortilla on the hot surface and cook about 1 to 1½ minutes, until it puffs when you "tickle" or touch it. Flip the tortilla and cook for another 30 seconds.

Transfer the cooked tortilla to a basket lined with a warm, moist cloth. Repeat until all the tortillas are cooked and serve immediately.

★ ★ ★

MASECA MASA HARINA VARIATION
Follow the directions for Corn Tortillas, but substitute 4 cups Maseca instant corn masa flour, 2⅔ cups plus 4 tablespoons warm water, and ½ teaspoon finely ground kosher or table salt.

★ ★ ★

FRESH MASA VARIATION
To make tortillas with fresh masa, use 1½ pounds of prepared fresh masa simple to make about sixteen 5½-inch corn tortillas or twenty-four 4-inch mini tortillas. Follow the directions for Corn Tortillas for shaping, pressing, and cooking. For standard tortillas, use about 1½ ounces of masa formed into 1½-inch balls. For mini tortillas, use about 1 ounce of masa formed into 1-inch balls. If the masa is a little dry and the tortillas are cracking on the edges, wet your hands with a little warm water when you roll out the dough. The cooking time is the same for either size. Be sure to store fresh masa purchased from a *tortilleria* in the refrigerator. Keep it well wrapped and use it within 2 days of purchase; otherwise the masa will ferment and spoil, even if refrigerated. Masa dough cannot be frozen.

FLOUR TORTILLAS

MAKES 8 (5½-INCH) FLOUR TORTILLAS

Flour tortillas are a mainstay of Tex-Mex cooking. You can see them rolling hot off the tortilla machines into baskets at many of the Tex-Mex restaurant chains (a show that kids love to watch), perfect for fajitas and juicy meats. One of my favorite ways to enjoy a flour tortilla is possible in Santa Fe only in August and September during the chile harvest. I'll peel and seed a fire-roasted fresh green chile, roll it, still steaming, in a warm fresh flour tortilla, and eat it up. Such a simple treat, yet so memorable.

These tortillas are very easy to make and so much fresher and lighter than any you can buy at the store. I've used bleached all-purpose flour for this recipe rather than bread flour. All-purpose flour has less gluten, so the dough is easier to roll out into thin tortillas that stay flat without shrinking back. As an alternative to making the dough from scratch, you can try Quaker Harina Preparada para Tortillas, a mix that contains all the ingredients in dry form that you need to make flour tortillas, including the fat. Just add water to prepare the dough. Some Hispanic markets stock it, or look for an online source.

★ ★ ★

To make the dough, in the work bowl of a food processor, add the flour and the vegetable shortening. Process 10 to 15 seconds to blend. With the machine running, add the warm salt water in a quick stream and process until a solid ball of moist, slightly sticky dough. If you think it needs more liquid, mix in 2 to 3 more tablespoons of warm water; the dough must be moist enough to roll out. Knead the dough a few times, then place it in a large bowl, cover with a clean kitchen towel, and let it rest for at least 1½ hours. Or place the dough in a large self-sealing plastic bag and let it rest in the refrigerator for the same amount of time.

Dust the work surface with a small amount of flour. Divide the dough into 8 balls of equal size, set them out on the work surface, and cover with a damp towel.

To shape the tortillas, with a narrow wooden rolling pin or dowel, roll out each ball into 5½-inch rounds that are about ¼ inch thick. Try not to blend in any extra flour, as that will make the tortillas tough. Keep the tortillas covered, and don't stack them.

To cook the tortillas, heat a dry heavy nonstick griddle or skillet over medium heat. Flip a tortilla onto the hot cooking surface and cook it until puffy and blistered with brown spots, about 1½ minutes. Flip it over and cook another 1½ minutes. Hold the tortillas in a basket covered with a warm towel. To reheat, cook briefly on both sides in a griddle or skillet over medium heat.

2 scant cups (450 grams) all-purpose flour (don't pack down), plus more for the work surface

½ cup solid vegetable shortening

1 scant teaspoon kosher salt dissolved in 1 cup of warm water

CRISPY TACOS, FLAUTAS, AND TAQUITOS

In Mexico, corn tortillas that are deep-fried until golden and crispy are called *tacos dorados* (fried tacos), the Mexican predecessor of the bright yellow, hard-shelled tacos of American fast-food fame. They're easy to make and fun to eat, whether as taco shells that you fill after frying or the delectable fried filled tubes known as flautas and taquitos.

★ ★ ★

CRISPY CORN TACO SHELLS

It's the crunchy contrast of hard shell and moist filling that does it for fans of fried tacos. Throughout the book are traditional and innovative fillings that make perfect partners to crispy fried tortillas. Try the take-out standard updated and refined as Classic Ground Beef with Guajillo Chiles (page 92), the smoky Tex-Mex allure of Barbecued Brisket (page 99), the fusion appeal of Thai Shrimp (page 59), or the unexpected meatiness of Portobello Mushrooms with Chipotle (page 24). These are just a few of the recipes that let you bring home the crunch without a trip to the drive-through.

You can purchase ready-to-fill crispy corn taco shells at most grocery stores. As the shells can quickly get stale and go rancid, buy them at a store with a very high turnover and buy just the amount you need for a meal, as they don't keep well. Of the national brands that I've tasted, those made by Taco Bell were the best and most reliable.

With not much effort, though, you can make taco shells that are tastier, fresher, and crisper than any you can buy and in just the size you need. And you don't even have to use tortillas. Wonton skins and egg roll wrappers, available at almost any supermarket, fry up into delicious shells ready for filling.

To make U-shaped taco shells from 5½-inch corn tortillas, a wire taco fry basket with slots that form multiple shells (anywhere from 4 to 8) at a time is the easiest way to shape and fry them. They're available at restaurant supply stores or online. Or, to create shells from 5½-inch corn tortillas, or wonton skins or egg roll wrappers cut into 5½-inch rounds, make a mold from a 5½-inch diameter metal can lid. Remove the lid from the can (preferably with a can opener that leaves a rounded dull edge on the lid). Fold the lid over a slim dowel—like a sharpening steel for knives—creating a slightly rounded (not sharply pinched) fold and a 1½-inch gap at the top.

CONTINUED ▶

For frying, in a deep fryer or large, heavy-bottomed pot, heat about 5 inches of canola oil over medium heat until it reaches 350°F on a deep-fat thermometer (monitor the temperature carefully; any hotter, and the shells will be too dark; any cooler, and they will be greasy).

To fry shells using a taco basket: Place a tortilla in each slot and submerge the basket in hot oil. Fry until a light golden brown, about 2 minutes. Remove from the hot oil and transfer to paper towels to drain.

To fry shells using a handmade mold: Wrap a taco-sized (5½-inch diameter) yellow corn tortilla, wonton skin, or egg roll wrapper around the outside of the mold, hold the mold with tongs, and submerge it into the hot oil. Fry the tortilla until a light golden brown, 1 minute. Fry a wonton skin or egg roll wrapper until it puffs up and turns light golden brown, 10 to 15 seconds for wonton skins and about 15 seconds for egg roll wrappers. Remove from the hot oil and transfer to paper towels to drain.

★ ★ ★

CRISPY APPETIZER AND HORS D'OEUVRE SHELLS
Make your own appetizer-size shells for elegant fillings like Lobster and Avocado (page 64), my Southwestern take on a grilled cheese sandwich, Rajas and Cheese (page 31), or any that you think shine as passed-around party fare. For small appetizer or hors d'oeuvre–size shells made from 4-inch corn tortillas or 3-inch round wonton skins or egg-roll wrappers cut into 3-inch rounds, make a mold from a 4-inch diameter metal can lid. Fold the lid over the handle of a wooden spoon, leaving the fold slightly rounded and a 1-inch gap at the top. Wrap a tortilla or wonton skin around the outside of the mold, hold the mold with tongs, and fry at 340°F and as directed for large shells, reducing frying times accordingly.

★ ★ ★

FLAUTAS AND TAQUITOS
These fried filled taco tubes are actually more Tex-Mex than Mex, but have become a popular Mexican street snack and restaurant favorite. Flautas (flutes) are larger, about the diameter of a cigar—about 4 to 5 inches long, and about 1 inch in diameter. Taquitos are smaller, more like a cigarillo—about 3 to 3½ inches long and ½ to ¾ inch

in diameter. Both flautas and taquitos are great choices for entertaining. Serve either as finger food, figuring 2 to 3 per person as an appetizer, or include them as part of a main course combination plate. In Mexico, both flautas and taquitos are usually made with corn tortillas, rarely with flour. For taquitos especially, it's very difficult to find flour tortillas thin enough to roll up into the proper tight little tubes and seal them securely.

At the end of many of the recipes in the book is a feature called Tortillas that notes fillings that work well as flautas or taquitos. Among the many delicious choices are all-vegetable Squash Blossoms with Green Chiles and Cheese (page 23) or Wild Forest Mushrooms with Garlic (page 25) to meat-based Yucatán Chicken with Achiote (page 48), Turkey with Mole (page 52), Pork Carnitas (page 78), or Braised Beef Short Ribs (page 96). In general, the best fillings are cheese based as they hold together and cook evenly. Meat or chicken should be shredded, rather than in big chunks, which can take too long to heat up, causing the tortilla to overfry and burn.

To make flautas and taquitos: Start with very fresh, very thin and pliable yellow corn tortillas—5½-inch rounds for flautas, about 4-inch rounds for taquitos.

Lay the tortilla on a work surface with the thicker side (if they are handmade) on the bottom for easier rolling. Spoon a line of filling on the tortilla about one-third the way up from the bottom edge and extending from side edge to side edge. You'll need about 2 tablespoons filling for flautas, 1½ tablespoons filling for taquitos. Begin rolling up from the bottom edge; the first roll should cover the filling. Continue rolling into a very tight cylinder, about 1 inch diameter for flautas, ¾ inch or less for taquitos. Stuff the ends with more filling using your fingers if necessary so the filling is firmly packed from one edge to the other (otherwise the oil will seep into the tube and make the filling greasy). For flautas, secure the edge of the tortilla with a toothpick. For taquitos, brush the edge of the tortilla with egg wash or water and press to seal.

To fry flautas and taquitos: In a deep fryer or large, heavy-bottomed pot, heat about 2½ inches of canola oil over medium heat until it reaches 350°F on a deep-fat thermometer (monitor the temperature carefully; any hotter, and the shells will be too dark; any cooler, and they will be greasy). Add the filled tubes in batches, if necessary, and fry until a light, golden brown, about 2 minutes for flautas, about 1 minute for taquitos. Remove from the hot oil with a slotted spoon and let drain on a plate lined with paper towels.

VEGETABLES

SQUASH BLOSSOMS WITH GREEN CHILES AND CHEESE

23

PORTOBELLO MUSHROOMS WITH CHIPOTLE

24

NOPALES EN BOLSO WITH VEGETABLES ESCABECHE

25

WILD FOREST MUSHROOMS WITH GARLIC

27

HUITLACOCHE AND ROASTED CORN

29

RAJAS AND CHEESE

31

ROASTED TOMATOES AND PUMPKIN SEED PESTO

33

MUSHROOMS WITH ROASTED CORN AND MARJORAM

34

SANTA FE–STYLE CALABACITAS

35

CHARRO BEANS WITH BLACKENED TOMATOES

36

SQUASH BLOSSOMS WITH GREEN CHILES AND CHEESE

MAKES 12 TACOS ~ HEAT LEVEL 3 ~ PREP TIME 1 HOUR

These tacos are a great way to enjoy the harvest from your late summer garden. The delicate orange-and-yellow flowers of squash plants are a prized treat throughout Mexico and the southwestern United States. Squash blossoms are an ideal partner to the green chiles grown in Hatch, New Mexico, widely available in the Southwest during late summer and early fall (see Sources, page 167). If you can't find New Mexico green chiles, you can use Anaheims, their slightly less robust California counterpart, found in produce markets throughout the country. I like to serve these tacos with a cold, citrusy beverage—margaritas for the adults and limeade for the kids. The tartness of the limes beautifully complements the warm, buttery cheese that oozes out of the taco with each bite.

* * *

Cut the prepared green and poblano chiles into ¼-inch-thick strips (rajas); set aside. Remove the stamens and pistils from the squash blossoms. Trim off any stems and cut into ½-inch julienne (matchsticks); reserve. Cut the blossoms in ½-inch julienne (matchsticks) and reserve.

In a large, heavy skillet, heat the oil over medium-high heat; add the onion and sauté until translucent, about 3 minutes. Add the garlic and salt and sauté for 30 seconds (don't let the garlic color or burn). Add the squash and juilenned squash-blossom stems (if any), decrease the heat to medium, and cook, stirring occasionally, until the squash begins to soften, about 4 minutes. Add the tomato, epazote, marjoram, basil, and the prepared green, poblano, jalapeño, and serrano chiles, stirring to mix all the ingredients well. Cook on medium heat for 2 minutes, stirring in the julienned squash blossoms during the last 30 seconds of cooking.

Remove from the heat, sprinkle with cheese, and serve immediately or keep warm in the pan until ready to serve.

To serve, lay the tortillas side by side, open face and overlapping on a platter. Divide the filling equally between the tortillas, top with salsa, and sprinkle with basil. Grab, fold, and eat right away. Or build your own taco: lay a tortilla, open face, in one hand. Spoon on some filling, top with salsa and basil, fold, and eat right away.

1 green chile, oil-roasted, peeled, cored, and seeded (page 153)

1 poblano chile, oil-roasted, peeled, cored, and seeded (page 153)

18 squash blossoms

2 tablespoons corn or other vegetable oil

1 white onion, cut into ¼-inch dice

2 cloves garlic, minced

½ teaspoon kosher salt

¾ pound yellow squash, halved lengthwise and sliced crosswise into ¼-inch-thick half-moons

1 yellow (or other color) tomato, cut into ¼-inch dice

2 tablespoons finely chopped fresh epazote (page 158)

2 tablespoons finely chopped fresh marjoram

1 tablespoon finely chopped fresh basil

1 jalapeño chile, stemmed and minced

1 serrano chile, stemmed and minced

2 cups grated queso Oaxaca (about 8 ounces), page 151

12 (5½-inch) soft white or yellow corn tortillas (page 13), for serving

Garnish: chopped fresh basil or cilantro leaves

TORTILLAS

Soft white or yellow corn tortillas or flautas (page 17)

ACCOMPANIMENTS

Tomatillo-Avocado Sauce (page 128), Salsa Fresca (page 130)

DRINKS

Margaritas, limeade, Mexican beer (such as Pacifico), sauvignon blanc

PORTOBELLO MUSHROOMS WITH CHIPOTLE

MAKES 8 TACOS ~ HEAT LEVEL 3 ~ PREP TIME 25 MINUTES

The earthy meatiness of portobello mushrooms pairs wonderfully with the smoky flavors of chipotle chiles. The mushrooms are sautéed in butter, which imparts a delicious nuttiness and helps the mushrooms brown. Toasted pine nuts or pumpkin seeds are a traditional and tasty garnish that increases the nuttiness of the dish. Small, fresh portobellos have tightly closed gills that are easy to slice through. The spongy gills of large portobellos must be scraped off with a spoon before the mushroom caps are sliced—but don't discard them. The gills can be tossed in the pan and cooked with the rest of the mushroom, adding color and depth of flavor.

* * *

Remove the mushroom stems, chop them, and reserve. If any of the mushrooms are large, scrape off the gills with a spoon and reserve. Cut the caps into ¼-inch-thick slices and reserve.

Preheat a heavy skillet large enough to hold the mushrooms in a single layer for about 2 minutes over medium-high heat. Melt the butter in the pan, then add the sliced mushroom caps, chopped stems, any reserved gills, minced garlic, salt, and pepper, and sauté until golden brown and caramelized, 8 to 10 minutes. You may need to cook the mushrooms in batches to be sure they brown and not steam from overcrowding. Add more butter as the mushrooms cook, if necessary, as they have a tendency to absorb all the butter from the pan.

Remove from the heat and mix in the chipotle puree and cilantro. Sprinkle on the cheese just to melt and serve immediately or keep warm until ready to serve.

To serve, lay the tortillas side by side, open face and overlapping on a platter. Divide the filling equally between the tortillas and top with salsa and pumpkin seeds. Grab, fold, and eat right away. Or build your own taco: lay a tortilla, open face, in one hand. Spoon on some filling, top with salsa and pine nuts, and eat right away.

1 pound portobello mushrooms (preferably small, with fresh, closed gills)

3 tablespooons (or more) unsalted butter

3 cloves garlic, minced

½ teaspoon kosher salt

Pinch of freshly ground black pepper

2 teaspoons chipotle puree (page 153)

1 tablespoon finely chopped fresh cilantro leaves

1 cup finely grated smoked mozzarella or smoked gouda cheese (about 4 ounces)

8 (5½-inch) soft yellow corn tortillas (page 13), for serving

Garnish: lightly toasted pine nuts or pumpkin seeds

TORTILLAS	ACCOMPANIMENTS	DRINKS
Soft yellow corn tortillas or flautas (page 17)	Mexican Crema (page 160), Tomatillo–Árbol Chile Salsa (page 135)	Dark beer, Tempranillo

NOPALES EN BOLSO WITH VEGETABLES ESCABECHE

MAKES 8 TACOS ~ HEAT LEVEL 3 ~ PREP TIME 50 MINUTES

By cooking the nopales—the flat paddles of the prickly pear cactus—at a controlled temperature in a sturdy self-sealing plastic bag (*en bolso*), we are able to infuse flavors slowly into the nopales and preserve a firmer texture and bright green color. The process is something like the restaurant technique *sous vide* (French for "under vacuum"), where food is vacuum packed, then cooked in a water bath to ensure even heat. You can't squeeze out all the air from a self-sealing plastic bag as with true *sous vide,* but this home adaptation still works well. You can find fresh nopales with spines removed at Hispanic markets, chain supermarkets located in Hispanic communities, or some specialty produce stores. The briny tartness of the vegetable escabeche (pickled vegetables) is balanced by the creaminess of the queso fresco, a slightly salty Mexican cheese that is similar in taste and texture to feta.

★ ★ ★

Cut the prepared green chiles into ¼-inch-thick strips (rajas); set aside.

To cook the nopales, fill a large pot halfway with water and heat it over medium heat until it reaches 165°F on an instant-read thermometer. Place the nopales, pickled jalapeños, ½ cup jalapeño liquid, garlic, coriander, cilantro, tarragon, thyme, salt, and olive oil in a large, heavy-duty (freezer-weight) self-sealing plastic bag. Squeeze out as much air as possible and then completely seal the bag. Place the bag in the hot water and cook for 25 minutes. When the nopales have finished cooking, let them sit in the brine in the bag for at least 1 hour, or overnight in the refrigerator.

When ready to assemble the filling, in a small skillet, heat the vegetable oil over medium heat and sauté the onion just until translucent (don't let it color), 2 to 3 minutes; set aside.

To make the escabeche, in a small saucepan, add the sugar and vinegar and bring to a boil over medium-high heat, stirring to dissolve the sugar completely. Add the sautéed onion and the Fresno chiles to the boiling liquid and cook for 5 minutes. Remove from the heat and let marinate at room temperature for at least 20 minutes. In a colander, strain the pickled vegetables, discarding the brine, and transfer the vegetables to a serving bowl.

CONTINUED ▶

2 green chiles, oil-roasted, peeled, cored, and seeded (page 154)

3 large fresh nopales (cactus paddles, about 7½ ounces total), spines removed (page 150)

3 canned whole pickled jalapeño chiles, drained (liquid reserved), halved lengthwise (page 154)

½ cup reserved pickled jalapeño chile liquid

3 cloves garlic, sliced

2 tablespoons coriander seed, toasted (page 164) and crushed

10 sprigs cilantro

1 sprig tarragon

1 sprig thyme

1½ teaspoons kosher salt

2 tablespoons lemon-infused olive oil (page 162)

2 tablespoons vegetable oil

1 white onion, sliced

½ cup sugar

2 cups white balsamic vinegar or unseasoned rice wine vinegar

2 Fresno chiles, stemmed and thinly sliced

TORTILLAS	ACCOMPANIMENTS	DRINKS	25
Soft yellow corn tortillas	Tomatillo-Avocado Sauce (page 128), Tomatillo–Árbol Chile Salsa (page 135)	Sémillon, Riesling, sauvignon blanc, a light Mexican beer (such as Sol or Corona)	

To finish the nopales, strain the contents of the plastic bag, reserving the nopales and discarding the brine. Slice the nopales crosswise into ¼-inch-thick strips (rajas), and combine with the pickled vegetables. Sprinkle with cheese and serve immediately or keep warm in a pan until ready to serve.

To serve, lay the tortillas side by side, open face and overlapping on a platter. Divide the filling equally between the tortillas and top with salsa and garnish. Grab, fold, and eat right away. Or build your own taco: lay a tortilla, open face, in one hand. Spoon on some filling, top with salsa and garnish, and eat right away.

1½ cups crumbled queso fresco (about 5 ounces), page 151

8 (5½-inch) soft yellow corn tortillas (page 13), for serving

Garnish: fresh flowering thyme or pickled sliced red chiles

WILD FOREST MUSHROOMS WITH GARLIC

MAKES 8 TACOS ~ HEAT LEVEL 0 ~ PREP TIME 30 MINUTES

During the summer monsoons in Santa Fe, we forage for wild mushrooms—mostly porcini-like varieties—in the high-altitude forests of the nearby Sangre de Cristo Mountains. We're always looking for new ways to use our earthy, robust bounty, and this woodsy taco is one of our favorites. Buy wild mushrooms in at least three colors or textures. They'll add interest to the filling and give you the option of mixing less costly types with the more pricey ones. Avoid shiitakes and enokis, which don't pair well with wild mushrooms (the enoki are too acrid, and the shiitake too powerful) or lobster mushrooms as they don't cook at the same rate and remain hard. Aim for a mix that is woodsy, rich, delicate, and very flavorful. Good substitutions for fresh wild mushrooms are a mix of dried wild mushrooms and fresh criminis, or dried porcini and thinly sliced portobellos.

★ ★ ★

Leave the mushrooms whole if they are small (about 1½ by ½ inches). For any that are large, cut them in pieces (with their stems) lengthwise to preserve their shape and match the size of the whole mushrooms. You want all the pieces to be of similar size.

Preheat a heavy skillet large enough to hold the mushrooms in a single layer for about 2 minutes over medium-high heat. Melt the butter in the pan and add the minced garlic and the mushrooms and sauté until the mushrooms are golden brown and caramelized, 8 to 10 minutes. You may need to cook the mushrooms in batches to be sure they brown and not steam from overcrowding. Add more butter as the mushrooms cook, if necessary, as they have a tendency to absorb all the butter from the pan. Add the truffle or porcini paste, and cook, stirring, for 30 seconds.

Remove from the heat and sprinkle with salt, pepper, and chives. Serve immediately or keep warm in the pan until ready to serve.

To serve, lay the tortillas side by side, open face and overlapping on a platter. Divide the filling equally between the tortillas and top with salsa and garnish. Grab, fold, and eat right away. Or build your own taco: lay a tortilla, open face, in one hand. Spoon on some filling, top with salsa and garnish, and eat right away.

1 pound mixed wild mushrooms (such as hen-of-the-woods, black or yellow chanterelles, or morels)

3 tablespoons (or more) unsalted butter

2 cloves garlic, minced

2 teaspoons Porcini Paste (page 161) or truffle paste (preferably black)

¾ teaspoon kosher salt

⅛ teaspoon freshly ground black pepper

1½ tablespoons very thinly sliced fresh chives

8 (5½-inch) soft yellow corn tortillas (page 13), for serving

Garnish: roasted onions, chopped fresh chives, or fresh watercress leaves

---

TORTILLAS

Soft yellow corn tortillas, crispy white corn tortilla shells (page 17), or taquitos (page 17)

ACCOMPANIMENTS

Cascabel Chile–Blackened Tomato Salsa (page 127), Mexican Crema (page 160)

DRINKS

Malbec, Barbaresco, pinot noir

27

HUITLACOCHE AND ROASTED CORN

MAKES 8 TACOS ~ HEAT LEVEL 4 ~ PREP TIME 1 HOUR

Huitlacoche is often referred to as "Mexican truffle" even though it is not related to truffles or mushrooms, but rather a fungus that grows naturally on corn in its wild state (spraying corn prevents the fungus). However, the flavor is pungent, earthy, and robust, all characteristics of true truffles. Highly prized in Mexico, fresh huitlacoche commands top prices when sold in the open markets there. Huitlacoche is almost impossible to find fresh in the United States. The federal government requires a special permit to grow it as a way to control infestation of the corn crop, as the spores are disseminated by air. It is usually available frozen and canned (see Sources, page 167). These tacos are hearty enough to be served by themselves, but also make a great side dish for a main course of beef.

★ ★ ★

Remove the mushroom stems, chop them, and reserve. If any of the mushrooms are large, scrape off the gills with a knife and reserve. Cut the caps into ¼-inch dice and reserve.

In a large, heavy skillet, melt the butter over medium-high heat and sauté the onion and bay leaf until the onion begins to caramelize, 6 to 8 minutes. Add the diced mushroom caps, chopped stems, any reserved gills, and salt and sauté until the mushrooms get soft and begin to brown, about 8 minutes. You may need to add more butter once the mushrooms have begun to cook as they have a tendency to absorb all the butter from the pan. Discard the bay leaf. Add the beer and cook until the liquid is reduced, about 2 minutes.

Stir in the garlic, serrano chiles, huitlacoche, huitlacoche liquid, tomatoes, water, chipotle puree, hoja santa, and epazote. Decrease the heat to medium-low and cook until the mixture begins to dry out, but still look slightly moist (like sandwich relish), 15 to 20 minutes. Add the beer and let it reduce for about 5 minutes; stir in the corn.

Remove from the heat and serve immediately or keep warm in the pan until ready to serve. To serve, lay the tortillas side by side, open face and overlapping on a platter. Divide the filling equally between the tortillas and top with salsa and cheese. Grab, fold, and eat right away. Or build your own taco: lay a tortilla, open face, in one hand. Spoon on some filling, top with salsa and cheese, and eat right away.

8 ounces portobello mushrooms

2 tablespoons unsalted butter

1 white onion, cut into ¼-inch dice

1 bay leaf

¾ teaspoon kosher salt

6 cloves garlic, dry-roasted (page 158)

2 serrano chiles, dry-roasted (page 153), stemmed and minced

1 cup frozen or canned huitlacoche (about 9 ounces), including any liquid rendered out in the package, coarsely chopped

2 Roma tomatoes, blackened (page 164) and cut into ¼-inch dice

½ cup water

½ teaspoon chipotle puree (page 153)

1 teaspoon finely chopped fresh hoja santa (page 159) or fresh tarragon

1 teaspoon finely chopped fresh epazote (page 158)

¼ cup dark beer

1 cup dry-roasted fresh corn kernels (page 157)

8 (5½-inch) soft yellow or white corn tortillas (page 13), for serving

Garnish: grated smoked mozzarella

TORTILLAS

Soft yellow or white corn tortillas or flautas (page 17)

ACCOMPANIMENTS

Mexican Crema (page 160), Tomatillo–Blackened Serrano Chile Salsa (page 135)

DRINK

Merlot

RAJAS AND CHEESE

MAKES 6 TACOS ~ HEAT LEVEL 5 ~ PREP TIME 30 MINUTES

A Southwest twist on the old classic of grilled cheese, this version is spicier and good comfort food. In the Southwest, the Spanish word rajas (slivers) has come to mean slim strips of cooked chile peppers or sweet bell peppers, here lifted with aromatic spices, a buttery cream, and slightly tangy cheese. When spooned into smaller tortillas, this enticingly rich filling makes a great appetizer or hors d'oeuvre taco. For a heartier snack, add chicken or beef. Large or small, with or without meat, they'll go as fast as you can make them. To reduce the heat level of this dish, leave out the seeds from the jalapeños.

★ ★ ★

Cut the prepared red bell peppers and poblano, green, and jalapeño chiles into ¼-inch-thick strips (rajas) and set aside in a large bowl.

In a large, heavy nonstick skillet, heat the oil over medium heat and sauté the onion until translucent, about 3 minutes. Decrease the heat to low, add the bell pepper and chile strips, then stir in the cilantro, oregano, salt, crema, queso Oaxaca, and grated Parmesan. Cook over low heat, stirring continuously (so the mixture doesn't brown or scorch), until the queso melts, about 5 minutes. It may be necessary to add a little water to the pan to keep the mixture from browning (the mixture may steam a little from the water).

Remove from the heat and serve immediately or keep warm in the pan until ready to serve.

To serve on a platter, lay the tortillas side by side, open face and overlapping on the platter. Divide the fillings equally between the tortillas and top with salsa and sun-dried tomatoes. Grab, fold, and eat right away. Or build your own taco: lay the tortilla, open face, in one hand. Spoon on some filling, top with salsa and sun-dried tomatoes, fold, and eat right away.

1½ large sweet red bell peppers, oil-roasted, peeled, cored, and seeded (page 154)

3 large poblano chiles, oil-roasted, peeled, cored, and seeded (page 154)

1 small green chile, oil-roasted, peeled, cored, and seeded (page 154)

3 jalapeño chiles, dry-roasted (page 154)

1 tablespoon vegetable oil

½ small white onion, cut into ¼-inch dice

2 teaspoons chopped fresh cilantro leaves

¼ teaspoon dried Mexican oregano, toasted (page 164)

Pinch of kosher salt

¾ cup Mexican Crema (or crème fraîche or natural sour cream), page 160

5 tablespoons grated queso Oaxaca or Chihuahua cheese (about 2 ounces), page 151

1½ tablespoons grated imported Parmesan cheese

6 (5½-inch) soft white corn tortillas (page 13)

Garnish: oil-packed sun-dried tomatoes, drained and cut in strips, or roasted cherry tomatoes

TORTILLAS	ACCOMPANIMENT	DRINKS	31
Soft white corn tortillas, flour tortillas, or 4-inch soft corn tortillas	Salsa Fresca (page 130)	Merlot, margaritas	

ROASTED TOMATOES AND PUMPKIN SEED PESTO

MAKES 8 TACOS ~ HEAT LEVEL I ~ PREP TIME I HOUR

This recipe is really all about the tomatoes. For the best results, make these tacos in summer when tomatoes are at their sweetest and seasonal best. Thicker-fleshed varieties, like Romas, work better for this filling as they give off less juice and cook down to a firmer consistency. After roasting, the tomato slices turn soft and crinkly. Thin shavings of buttery, piquant Spanish Manchego cheese makes a wonderful addition, as do leaves of peppery arugula or sprigs of cilantro. Pumpkin seeds are available toasted, which deepens their flavor, or you can easily toast them yourself in a hot, dry skillet. These tacos can easily be served in place of a salad course for a dinner party. The pesto will hold for one week in the refrigerator and shines with pastas, seafood, or meat dishes. For a quick version, substitute about four ounces purchased roasted tomatoes, stocked at specialty markets. Look for them in bulk where olives are sold, packed with herbs and a bit of oil.

1 pound small Roma tomatoes, cored

2 teaspoons kosher salt

½ teaspoon sugar

6 poblano chiles, oil-roasted, peeled, cored, and seeded (page 154)

¾ cup pumpkin seeds, lightly toasted (page 164)

¾ teaspoon green chile powder (page 151)

2 teaspoons lemon-infused olive oil (page 162)

1 tablespoon fresh lime juice

1 cup loosely packed, coarsely chopped fresh cilantro leaves

8 (5½-inch) soft yellow corn tortillas (page 13)

Garnish: chopped fresh basil or mint leaves

★ ★ ★

Preheat the oven to 200°F. Line a baking sheet with parchment paper.

Halve the tomatoes across their midsections and gently squeeze the halves to release seeds and excess juice (the tomatoes will cook faster). Slice the tomatoes thinly. In a bowl, toss the slices with ½ teaspoon of the salt and the sugar. Spread the slices in a single layer (so the tomatoes are evenly exposed to the heat) on the prepared baking sheet. Roast for at least 2 hours, or until the tomatoes are about three-fourths dehydrated and the flesh is the consistency of a roasted bell pepper (they'll resemble soft sundried tomatoes). The slices will shrink by about half during roasting; no need to turn them.

Remove from the oven and set aside until at cool room temperature.

Cut the prepared poblano chiles into ¼-inch-thick strips (rajas); set aside.

Meanwhile, to prepare the pesto, in the work bowl of a food processor fitted with the metal blade, combine the pumpkin seeds, chile powder, olive oil, lime juice, cilantro, and remaining 1½ teaspoons salt. Process until the consistency of ground almond butter (a little rougher than peanut butter) or as you prefer.

To serve, lay the tortillas side by side, open face and overlapping on a platter. Divide the pesto equally between the tortillas and top with roasted tomato slices, chile strips, salsa, and basil. Grab, fold, and eat right away. Or build your own taco: lay a tortilla, open face, in one hand. Spoon on some pesto, top with tomato slices, chile strips, salsa, and basil, and eat right away.

TORTILLAS	ACCOMPANIMENTS	DRINKS	
Soft yellow corn tortillas or crispy yellow corn tortilla shells (page 17)	Tomatillo–Blackened Serrano Chile Salsa (page 135), Mexican Crema (page 160)	Dry Riesling, sauvignon blanc	33

MUSHROOMS WITH ROASTED CORN AND MARJORAM

MAKES 6 TACOS ~ HEAT LEVEL 2 ~ PREP TIME 30 MINUTES

The combination of sweet, lightly smoked corn and rich, earthy mushrooms is one of the great flavor marriages of Mexican food. In this filling, inspired by one of my favorite salsa recipes in *The Great Salsa Book*, the fresh corn kernels are dry-roasted to capture the sweet corn flavor and infuse them with an appetizing, smoky perfume. Dry roasting is one of the great culinary techniques that give Mexican cuisine its distinctiveness and meaning, and one easily mastered at home. Very simply and effectively, it intensifies and concentrates flavors and imparts the smoky, primordial quality that is characteristic of so many Mexican dishes. Beyond corn, the technique is also used for garlic, tomatoes, and onions, for fresh and dried chiles, and for seeds and nuts.

★ ★ ★

Cut the prepared poblano chiles into ¼-inch-thick strips (rajas); set aside.

Preheat a heavy skillet large enough to hold the mushrooms in a single layer for about 2 minutes over medium-high heat. Melt the butter in the pan, then add the mushrooms, garlic, salt, and pepper, and sauté until the mushrooms are golden brown and caramelized, 6 to 8 minutes.

Remove the pan from the heat and stir in the corn, olive oil, chipotle puree, lime juice, cilantro, and marjoram. Serve immediately or keep warm in the pan until ready to serve.

To serve, lay the tortillas side by side, open face and overlapping on a platter. Divide the filling equally between the tortillas and top with salsa and basil. Grab, fold, and eat right away. Or build your own taco: lay a tortilla, open face, in one hand. Spoon on some filling, top with salsa and basil, fold, and eat right away.

2 medium poblano chiles, oil-roasted, peeled, cored, and seeded (page 154)

3 tablespoons (or more) butter

6 ounces portobello mushrooms (preferably small, with fresh, closed gills), cut into ¼-inch-thick slices with stems

1½ ounces shiitake mushrooms, stemmed, cut into ¼-inch-thick slices

2 cloves garlic, minced

½ teaspoon kosher salt

¼ teaspoon freshly ground black pepper

1 cup fresh corn kernels, dry-roasted (page 157)

1 tablespoon olive oil (preferably Spanish)

1 teaspoon chipotle puree (page 153)

1 teaspoon fresh lime juice

2 teaspoons loosely packed chopped fresh cilantro leaves

1 teaspoon chopped fresh marjoram

8 (5½-inch) soft white corn tortillas (page 13), for serving

Garnish: julienned fresh basil or toasted pine nuts (page 164)

TORTILLAS	ACCOMPANIMENTS	DRINKS
Soft white corn tortillas or flautas (page 17)	Chipotle Sauce (page 126), Green Chile Sauce (page 132), sun-dried tomato pesto	Pinot noir, Tempranillo

SANTA FE—STYLE CALABACITAS

MAKES 8 TACOS ~ HEAT LEVEL 2 ~ PREP TIME 40 MINUTES

Calabacitas (Spanish for "little squashes") is a traditional side dish that I've converted into a delicious taco filling that celebrates summer bounty. All squash are native to the New World and, with corn, beans, and chiles, one of the "four magic plants" (as I call them) of the Southwest. Squash and corn not only like to grow together in the garden, they have a natural ecology that helps fix the nitrogen content of the soil, and they taste wonderful when cooked together. You can add fresh or frozen baby lima beans or fresh or dried green beans here for added color and nutrition. Be sure to cook the vegetables very slowly to capture all their natural sweetness and complexity.

★ ★ ★

Cut the prepared green chiles into ¼-inch-thick strips (rajas); set aside.

In a large, heavy skillet, heat the oil over medium-high heat and sauté the onion and marjoram until the onion begins to caramelize, about 5 minutes. Add the garlic, cover the pan, and cook 5 minutes more. Add the yellow and zucchini squashes and corn kernels and cook, tightly covered, until the squash is tender, about 15 minutes. Add the chile, tomato, and cilantro, and season with salt and pepper. Cook, uncovered, another 2 minutes so the flavors can blend.

Remove from the heat and serve immediately or keep warm in the pan until ready to serve.

To serve, lay the tortillas side by side, open face and overlapping on a platter. Divide the filling equally between the tortillas and top with salsa and pesto. Grab, fold, and eat right away. Or build your own taco: lay a tortilla, open face, in one hand. Spoon on some filling, top with salsa and pesto, fold, and eat right away.

1 medium green chile, oil-roasted, peeled, cored, and seeded (page 154)

2 tablespoons vegetable oil

1 medium yellow onion, halved and thinly sliced

1 tablespoon plus 1 teaspoon chopped fresh marjoram

3 cloves garlic, minced

¼ pound yellow squash, halved lengthwise and cut crosswise into ¼-inch-thick half-moons

¼ pound zucchini, halved lengthwise and cut crosswise into ¼-inch-thick half-moons

1 cup fresh corn kernels (from about 1 ear fresh corn)

1 small Roma tomato, cored, seeded, and diced

1 tablespoon chopped fresh cilantro leaves

Kosher salt and freshly ground black pepper

8 (5½-inch) soft white corn tortillas (page 13), for serving

Garnish: pumpkin seed pesto (page 33) or basil pesto

TORTILLAS	ACCOMPANIMENTS	DRINKS	35
Soft white or yellow corn tortillas	Chipotle Sauce (page 126), Green Chile Sauce (page 132), Mexican Crema (page 160)	Margaritas, chardonnay	

CHARRO BEANS WITH BLACKENED TOMATOES

MAKES 8 TACOS ~ HEAT LEVEL I ~ PREP TIME 2½ HOURS

The word *charro* refers to the original cowboys of the New World, the Mexican and Spanish men who handled the cattle on the large ranches of Mexico and California, and then Texas and the Southwest. The entire cow culture—the hats, saddles, ropes, boots—was brought here by Spanish explorers and settlers. These men lived a nomadic life that revolved around the search for the best seasonal pastures for their herds. Meals were always prepared over open campfires, giving food a smokiness that is forever associated with cowboy cooking. Beans were a common side dish, and the smoked salt in this recipe helps to replicate those robust and smoky flavors. The beans will hold for one week in the refrigerator, and their versatility makes them handy to have around.

★ ★ ★

To cook the beans, in a large pot, simmer the beans, garlic, ½ onion, and the 6½ cups water over medium-low heat, partially covered, until the beans are almost falling apart, 2 to 4 hours. Add water as necessary during cooking so the mixture doesn't dry out. After the beans are cooked, drain the bean liquid into a saucepan and return the beans to the large pot. Over medium heat, reduce the liquid until it is thickened (not too much liquid will be left), about 10 minutes; reserve.

Meanwhile, cut the remaining ½ onion into ¼-inch dice. In a skillet, heat the oil over medium-high heat and sauté the diced onion until it begins to caramelize, about 5 minutes. Add the garlic and sauté for 30 seconds (don't let the garlic burn); set aside.

Into the pot of cooked beans, stir in the sautéed onion and garlic, chiles, tomatoes, tomato paste, chipotle puree, smoked salt, oregano, cilantro, and the thickened bean juice, and cook over medium heat for 20 minutes. Remove from the heat and serve immediately, or keep warm in the pan until ready to serve.

To serve, lay the tortillas side by side, open face and overlapping on a platter. Divide the filling equally between the tortillas and top with salsa and jerky strips. Grab, fold, and eat right away. Or build your own taco: lay a tortilla, open face, in one hand. Spoon on some filling, top with salsa and jerky strips, and eat right away.

1 cup dried pinto beans, rinsed 3 times and picked over for rocks

3 cloves garlic

1 small white onion, halved

6½ cups water

2 tablespoons olive oil (preferably Spanish)

2 cloves garlic, minced

2 jalapeño chiles, dry-roasted (page 154)

1 pound tomatoes, blackened (page 164) and cut into ¼-inch dice

1 teaspoon tomato paste

¼ teaspoon chipotle puree (page 153)

½ teaspoon smoked salt (page 163)

¼ teaspoon dried Mexican oregano, toasted and ground (page 165)

1 tablespoon chopped fresh cilantro leaves

8 (5½-inch) soft yellow corn tortillas (page 13), for serving

Garnish: strips of soft beef or game jerky (lightly steamed, if dry)

TORTILLAS	ACCOMPANIMENT	DRINK
Soft yellow corn tortillas	Tomatillo–Árbol Chile Salsa (page 135)	Dark beer

CHICKEN AND FOWL

CHICKEN TINGA

40

CHICKEN WITH MOLE VERDE FROM PUEBLA

41

SONORAN CHICKEN WITH NOPALES

43

CHICKEN WITH RAJAS AND CORN

45

CHICKEN WITH APPLES AND GOAT CHEESE

46

CHICKEN WITH CHORIZO

48

YUCATÁN CHICKEN WITH ACHIOTE

50

DUCK WITH PECAN PIPIÁN

51

TURKEY WITH MOLE

53

ESCABECHE TURKEY WITH PICKLED VEGETABLES

55

CHICKEN TINGA

MAKES 15 TACOS ~ HEAT LEVEL 7 ~ PREP TIME 1 HOUR

The Spanish word *tinga* means "unruly" or "messy." But there is nothing messy about the wonderful flavors of this dish with its layers of smoky and sweet. The browned chicken has accents of balsamic vinegar, roasted sweet peppers, and chiles—a sort of Mexican chicken cacciatore. I consider it one of Mexican cuisine's top ten classic dishes. Tinga tacos are a perennial favorite in northern New Mexico and can have other fillings beside chicken. In addition to tacos or burritos, this filling—really a homey soul-satisfying stew—can be served in a bowl over rice. It also makes a great *bocadillo*, a Mexican sandwich served on a square crispy roll. To reduce the heat level of this dish, decrease or leave out the chipotle puree.

* * *

Cut the prepared poblano chile and bell pepper into ¼-inch-thick strips (rajas); set aside.

In a large bowl, toss the chicken strips with the chile powder, salt, and black pepper and let marinate for 20 minutes.

Toward the end of the marinating time, in a large, heavy skillet, heat the oil over medium-high heat. Add the chicken strips and sauté until just barely cooked through, about 5 minutes. Remove the sausage from its casings, crumble it, and add it to the skillet along with the poblano chile strips, red bell pepper strips, and onion. Sauté, stirring occasionally, until the sausage begins to brown, about 4 minutes. Decrease heat to medium. Add the garlic, chipotle puree, juice, tomatoes, vinegar, oregano, and brown sugar and cook, stirring occasionally, until almost all of the liquid has cooked down, about 6 minutes. The mixture should be moist but not wet.

Remove from the heat and serve immediately, or keep warm in the pan until ready to serve.

For crispy tacos, divide the lettuce slaw then the filling equally between the crispy shells, top with salsa and garnish, and arrange in a taco holder. Or, lean the filled shells in a row, propped upright, on a platter. Eat right away. To build your own, spoon some slaw and filling in a crispy shell, top with salsa and garnish, and eat right away.

1 poblano chile, oil-roasted, peeled, cored, and seeded (page 154)

1 sweet red bell pepper, oil-roasted, peeled, cored, and seeded (page 154)

2 pounds boneless, skinless chicken breasts, cut into 1-inch strips

1 tablespoon red jalapeño chile powder (page 151)

2 teaspoons kosher salt

1 teaspoon black pepper

3 tablespoons canola oil

12 ounces jalapeño-chicken sausage

1 large white onion, halved and cut into ¼-inch-thick slices

15 cloves garlic, dry-roasted (page 158) and mashed

¾ cup chipotle puree (page 153)

12 ounces spicy vegetable juice

12 ounces tomatoes, blackened (page 164) and cut into ¼-inch dice

½ cup balsamic vinegar

1 tablespoon dried Mexican oregano, toasted and ground

3 tablespoons dark brown sugar

15 (5½-inch) crispy yellow corn tortilla shells (page 17)

Garnish: Iceberg Lettuce Garnish (page 144) or chopped fresh cilantro

---

TORTILLAS

Crispy yellow corn tortilla shells (page 17), soft yellow corn tortillas, or flautas (page 17)

ACCOMPANIMENTS

Salsa Fresca (page 130), Roasted Pineapple–Habanero Chile Salsa (page 129)

DRINKS

Margaritas, coco locos, piña coladas

CHICKEN WITH MOLE VERDE FROM PUEBLA

MAKES 5 QUARTS OF MOLE SAUCE, AND 12 TACOS
HEAT LEVEL 6 ~ PREP TIME 3 HOURS

The town of Puebla, a serene and peaceful oasis about one hour south from the congestion and commotion of Mexico City, is known for its charming inns that serve a rich array of traditional dishes. The most famous mole (the word is from a pre-Columbian language of Mexico and means a sauce that is blended with more than one chile or ingredient) originated in the kitchen of a large, wealthy Puebla convent with chocolate as its most acclaimed ingredient. But there are six other moles from the region. This filling, the green mole that uses all fresh herbs and fresh green chiles, is one of the simpler ones and the one that I usually eat for breakfast at the market—one huge bowl of chicken mole verde with fresh warm corn tortillas. Admittedly, it is a little time-consuming, but your effort will be rewarded with enough mole sauce to use for these tacos and many others. Leftover mole will keep in the refrigerator for at least a week, or you can freeze it for up to 3 months. This sauce makes a tasty complement to chicken, turkey, fish, and pork.

★ ★ ★

To prepare the mole, cut the prepared poblano chiles into ¼-inch-thick strips (rajas); set aside along with the serrano and jalapeño chiles.

Fill a large bowl with ice water and have ready. Bring a large pot of salted water to a boil over high heat. Drop in the husked tomatillos and boil 5 minutes. Remove from the heat. With a slotted spoon, transfer the tomatillos to the ice-water bath; let cool.

In a large, heavy skillet, heat 2 tablespoons of the oil over medium-high heat and sauté the diced onion just until translucent, 3 to 5 minutes. Decrease the heat to medium-low. Add the stock, prepared poblano chiles, serrano chiles, jalapeño chiles, garlic, salt, sugar, and coriander and cook, stirring occasionally, until the mixture is slightly thickened and coats a wooden spoon, about 20 minutes. Stir in the shredded lettuce, hoja santa, cilantro, and parsley, and cook 5 more minutes.

Puree the mixture in a blender and pass it through a medium-mesh sieve. Refry the sauce: In a large, heavy nonstick skillet, heat the remaining 1 tablespoon of oil over high heat until almost smoking. Add the sauce, remove from the heat, and stir to blend. Add the ground pumpkin seeds to thicken the sauce. If the sauce is too thick and becoming pasty, stir in a little hot water to thin it out. Keep warm.

CONTINUED ▶

MOLE VERDE SAUCE

15 poblano chiles, oil-roasted, peeled, cored, and seeded (page 154)

5 serrano chiles, oil-roasted, peeled, cored, and seeded (page 154)

5 jalapeño chiles, oil-roasted, peeled, cored, and seeded (page 154)

2 pounds tomatillos, husked and rinsed

3 tablespoons vegetable oil

1 white onion, cut into ¼-inch dice

4 cups chicken stock

8 cloves garlic, dry-roasted (page 158)

2 teaspoons kosher salt

½ teaspoon sugar

½ teaspoon coriander seed, toasted and ground (page 164)

2 cups shredded romaine lettuce leaves

3 fresh hoja santa leaves, stemmed, deveined, and chopped (page 159) or ¼ cup chopped fresh tarragon leaves

Leaves from 1 bunch fresh cilantro

½ cup chopped fresh flat-leaf parsley

1 cup pumpkin seeds, lightly toasted and ground (page 164)

TORTILLAS

Soft yellow corn tortillas

ACCOMPANIMENTS

Salsa Fresca (page 130),
Mexican Crema (page 160)

DRINK

Sauvignon blanc

To prepare the filling, in a large saucepot, add all the ingredients except the chicken breasts. Cook over medium-low heat until the flavors blend, about 30 minutes. Decrease the heat to low, add the chicken breasts, and gently simmer until the chicken is thoroughly cooked, about 25 minutes. It's important to let the chicken cool in the liquid to keep it more moist. When cool enough to handle, shred the cooled chicken with your hands into a bowl.

In a saucepan, add 3 cups of the mole verde and the shredded chicken and reheat over medium-low heat.

Remove from the heat and serve immediately or keep warm in the pan until ready to serve.

To serve, lay the tortillas side by side, open face and overlapping on a platter. Divide the filling equally between the tortillas and top with salsa. Grab, fold, and eat right away.

Or build your own taco: lay a tortilla, open face, in one hand. Spoon on some filling, top with salsa, fold, and eat right away.

CHICKEN FILLING

8 cups chicken stock

1 head garlic, halved

½ tablespoon coriander seed, toasted and ground (page 164)

½ teaspoon freshly ground black pepper

1 bay leaf

1 teaspoon kosher salt

½ bunch flat-leaf parsley

1 white onion, cut into ½-inch dice

2 pounds boneless, skinless chicken breasts

12 (5½-inch) soft yellow corn tortillas (page 13), for serving

SONORAN CHICKEN WITH NOPALES

MAKES 8 TACOS ~ HEAT LEVEL 2–3 ~ PREP TIME 30 MINUTES

This recipe makes use of nopales cooked *sous vide*—under vacuum, a technique from the professional kitchen that I've modified here for home cooks (see also Nopales en Bolso with Vegetables Escabeche, page 28). Nopales—cactus leaves—have a wonderful texture and fresh flavor almost like fresh green beans or green squash. In Mexico, they grow wild everywhere, available for the picking. The most amazing place to see nopales is at the central market of Mexico City, one of the truly great markets of the world. Arranged in circles are huge, round burlap bags, five feet tall by four feet wide. Each bag holds hundreds of nopales, and workers handle sixty to seventy-five bags simultaneously. Women whittle away at mountains of nopales with long, sharp knives, trimming off their sharp spines in seconds while gossiping with their neighbors, stopping only to sell to shoppers. The enormous amount of nopales sold underscores how important they are to the daily diet.

★ ★ ★

To cook the nopales, fill a large pot halfway with water and heat it over medium heat until it reaches 165°F on an instant-read thermometer. Place the nopales, lime juice, olive oil, ½ teaspoon of the salt, pepper, thyme, and water in a large, heavy-duty (freezer-weight) self-sealing plastic bag. Squeeze out as much air as possible and then completely seal the bag. Place the bag in hot water and cook for 20 minutes. Remove the bag from the water and let sit in an ice bath until cool. When cooled, empty the contents of the plastic bag into a strainer set over a bowl, reserving the cooled nopales strips and discarding the liquid and thyme sprigs.

In a spice grinder, grind together the toasted coriander and cumin seed, the remaining 1 teaspoon salt, chile powder, and toasted pumpkin seeds to a fine powder. Transfer to a flat dish and combine with the lemon-infused oil and lemon zest. Dredge the chicken breasts in the seasoning mixture.

Preheat the oven to 350°F. In a large, heavy skillet, heat the vegetable oil over medium heat. Sauté the seasoned breasts on both sides until lightly browned and slightly crusty, about 3 to 4 minutes per side. The breasts will brown quickly, so watch them carefully as they cook.

CONTINUED ▶

3 large fresh nopales (cactus paddles, about 7½ ounces total), spines removed and sliced into long ½-inch-thick strips (page 150)

Juice of 1 lime

3 tablespoons olive oil (preferably Spanish)

1½ teaspoons kosher salt

Pinch of freshly ground black pepper

2 sprigs fresh thyme

½ cup water

1 teaspoon coriander seed, toasted (page 164)

1 teaspoon cumin seed, toasted (page 164)

¼ teaspoon chipotle chile powder

2 tablespoons pumpkin seeds, lightly toasted (page 164)

1 teaspoon lemon-infused olive oil (page 162)

½ teaspoon grated lemon zest

2 pounds boneless, skinless chicken breast

2 tablespoons vegetable oil

TORTILLAS	ACCOMPANIMENTS	DRINKS	43
Soft yellow corn tortillas	Tomatillo–Blackened Serrano Chile Salsa (page 135), Mexican Crema (page 160)	Pinot noir, margaritas	

Transfer the browned chicken breasts to a baking sheet and bake until they are thoroughly cooked, but not dry, about 7 minutes. Remove from the oven and slice the breasts crosswise on the diagonal into ⅓-inch-thick pieces.

To serve, lay the tortillas side by side, open face and overlapping on a platter. Divide the lettuce and chicken strips equally between the tortillas and top with nopales strips, grated radish, cheese, and salsa. Grab, fold, and eat right away. Or build your own taco: lay a tortilla, open face, in one hand. Spoon on some lettuce and chicken, top with nopales, grated radish, cheese, and salsa, fold, and eat right away.

8 (5½-inch) soft yellow corn tortillas (page 13), for serving

Garnish: Iceberg Lettuce Garnish (page 144), finely grated radish, and grated queso fresco

CHICKEN WITH RAJAS AND CORN

MAKES 6 TACOS ~ HEAT LEVEL 4 ~ PREP TIME 30 MINUTES

This quick, convenient recipe is a Southwestern take on a popular Southern classic—sweet summer corn and barbecued chicken. Sauteing the chicken to brown the surface deepens both color and flavor and approximates the Mexican technique of cooking on a comal or griddle. To cut down on the preparation time for this recipe, use a good, all-natural rotisserie chicken from the grocery store.

★ ★ ★

Cut the prepared poblano chile, red bell pepper, and jalapeño chiles (with seeds) into ¼-inch-thick strips (rajas); set aside.

In a large, heavy skillet, heat the oil over medium-high heat and sauté the diced onion until it begins to caramelize, about 5 minutes. Reduce the heat to medium-low. Add the reserved chile and bell pepper, the shredded cooked chicken, salt, corn, jalapeños, and Tabasco and gently heat (you may need to add about ¼ cup water to keep the mixture from drying out).

Remove from the heat and serve immediately or keep warm in the pan until ready to serve.

To serve, lay the tortillas side by side, open face and overlapping on a platter. Divide the filling equally between the tortillas and top with salsa and garnish. Grab, fold, and eat right away. Or build your own taco: lay a tortilla, open face, in one hand. Spoon on some filling, top with salsa and garnish, fold, and eat right away.

½ poblano chile, oil-roasted, peeled, cored, and seeded (page 154)

½ sweet red bell pepper, oil-roasted, peeled, cored, and seeded (page 154)

2 jalapeño chiles, dry-roasted (page 154)

2 tablespoons vegetable oil

1 small white onion, cut into ¼-inch dice

2¼-pound roasted chicken, skinned and shredded (about 1½ pounds picked meat)

½ teaspoon kosher salt

1 cup fresh corn kernels (from about 1 large ear fresh corn), dry-roasted (page 157)

1½ tablespoons Tabasco sauce

6 (5½-inch) soft yellow corn tortillas (page 13), for serving

Garnish: Pickled Onions with Sweet Bell Peppers (page 146)

TORTILLAS

Soft yellow corn tortillas

ACCOMPANIMENTS

Green Chile Sauce (page 132), Chipotle Sauce (page 126), Salsa Fresca (page 130)

DRINKS

Merlot, Malbec

45

CHICKEN WITH APPLES AND GOAT CHEESE

MAKES 8 TACOS ~ HEAT LEVEL <1 ~ PREP TIME 30 MINUTES

Here in New Mexico, we have a number of really good goat-cheese producers who sell their products at farmer's markets. Spanish settlers originally introduced goats to the region along with the craft of making goat cheese. For Mexican recipes, I prefer the flavor of goat cheese to American cheeses made with cow's milk. Mexican cooking is rich and needs the counterpoint of a sharp cheese for balance and lively taste. Cow's milk cheeses are usually too creamy and flat in flavor, absorb too much of the flavor accents from a dish, and lack a certain acidity and sharpness common to Mexican cheeses. New Mexico also has great apples, as good as those I grew up with in New England. At an elevation of 7,000 feet, Santa Fe experiences very cold nights in the fall that "crisp" the apples and set the juices. The sweet juiciness of apples is a perfect match to the mild creaminess, tang, and richness of goat cheese. You can use the goat cheese as a garnish, if you prefer, rather than mixing it into the filling.

* * *

Cut the prepared poblano chile into ¼-inch-thick strips (rajas); set aside. Mash the garlic and about 1 teaspoon salt together with the side of knife to make a paste; set aside.

Season the chicken breasts with a little salt. In a large, heavy skillet, heat the oil over medium-high heat. Brown the chicken pieces lightly on both sides, 2½ to 3 minutes per side. Decrease the heat to medium; add the garlic paste and sauté 30 seconds (do not let it burn). Stir in the green chile powder, oregano, and apple cider. Cook, uncovered, until the liquid is reduced to a syrup and the chicken is cooked through, about 6 minutes. Remove from the heat. Slice the chicken breasts into ¼-inch-thick strips and return the strips to the pan along with the apples and the rajas. Remove from the heat, sprinkle with cheese, and serve immediately or keep warm in the pan until ready to serve.

To serve, lay the tortillas side by side, open face and overlapping on a platter. Divide the filling equally between the tortillas and top with salsa and garnish. Grab, fold, and eat right away. Or build your own taco: lay a tortilla, open face, in one hand. Spoon on some filling, top with salsa and garnish, fold, and eat right away.

1 poblano chile, oil-roasted, peeled, cored, and seeded (page 154)

2 cloves garlic, minced

Kosher salt

1½ pounds boneless, skinless chicken breasts

2 tablespoons vegetable oil

2 teaspoons green chile powder (page 151)

¾ teaspoon dried Mexican oregano, toasted and ground (page 164)

1 cup unfiltered apple cider

1½ cups cored, peeled, thinly sliced Gala, Jonathan, or Fuji apples (about 2 apples)

6 ounces semidry goat cheese, crumbled

8 (5½-inch) flour tortillas (page 16), for serving

Garnish: lightly toasted pine nuts (page 164), basil pesto, sun-dried-tomato cheese spread, or grated cheese like asadero, Cotija, Romano, or Parmesan

TORTILLAS	ACCOMPANIMENT	DRINKS
Soft yellow corn tortillas or flour tortillas	Tomatillo–Árbol Chile Salsa (page 135)	Dry Riesling, sauvignon blanc, pinot gris

CHICKEN WITH CHORIZO

MAKES 8 TACOS ~ HEAT LEVEL 3
PREP TIME 45 MINUTES (PLUS 1 HOUR FOR MARINATING)

Chorizo is usually made from pork, but you can find wonderful beef or chicken chorizo as well as an excellent vegetarian chorizo made from tofu. I've had a delicious green chorizo in Puebla that was a regional specialty composed of fresh green herbs and chiles blended with pork. The green marinade for the chicken plays wonderfully against the red chile of the chorizo. These hearty tacos are also great served with queso fresco or grated Cheddar or gouda cheese. Quail eggs fried sunny-side up makes a tasty garnish, if you like.

* * *

In the jar of a blender, place the water, lime juice, chiles, cilantro, garlic, green chile powder, cumin, coriander, oregano, salt, parsley, and green onions and puree until smooth. Have the chicken strips ready in a large bowl. Pour the marinade over the chicken and let sit for at least 1 hour in the refrigerator.

If the chorizo is in links, slit open the casings, remove the filling (discard the casings), and break it up with your hands. Bulk sausage is ready to use. In a large, heavy skillet, heat the oil over medium heat and sauté the onion until caramelized, about 4 minutes.

Add the chorizo to the onion and cook, stirring occasionally, until the chorizo is thoroughly cooked, about 7 minutes. Remove from the pan and set aside, leaving any fat in the pan.

To cook the chicken, remove the strips from the marinade and drain off any excess liquid. In the same pan as the chorizo mixture, sauté the chicken, turning once or twice, until a light golden color and thoroughly cooked, about 9 minutes.

Remove from the heat and serve immediately or keep warm in the pan until ready to serve.

To serve, divide the filling equally between the crispy shells, top with salsa, and arrange in a taco holder. Or, lean the filled shells in a row, propped upright, on a platter. Eat right away. To build your own, spoon some filling in a crispy shell, top with salsa, and eat right away.

½ cup water

1 tablespoon fresh lime juice

1 poblano chile, stemmed

1 jalapeño chile, stemmed

Leaves from 1 bunch fresh cilantro

2 cloves garlic

1 teaspoon green chile powder (page 151)

½ teaspoon cumin seed, toasted and ground (page 164)

½ teaspoon coriander seed, toasted and ground (page 164)

¼ teaspoon dried Mexican oregano, toasted and ground (page 164)

1 teaspoon kosher salt

¼ cup chopped fresh flat-leaf parsley

1 bunch green onions, root ends trimmed and cut in big pieces

1¼ pounds boneless, skinless chicken breasts, cut in ½-inch-wide strips

6 ounces Mexican pork chorizo, bulk or links

1 tablespoon vegetable oil

½ white onion, thinly sliced

8 (5½-inch) crispy yellow corn tortilla shells (page 17), for serving

TORTILLAS	ACCOMPANIMENT	DRINKS
Crispy yellow corn tortilla shells	Salsa Fresca (page 130)	Dark beer, chilled rosé

YUCATÁN CHICKEN WITH ACHIOTE

MAKES 8 TACOS ~ HEAT LEVEL 3
PREP TIME 20 MINUTES (PLUS 1 HOUR FOR MARINATING)

Achiote paste is a distinctive staple marinade of the Yucatán peninsula that infuses food with a brick-red hue, a part bitter–part acidic flavor, and an earthy intensity that lingers on the palate. It's usually combined with the bitter orange of the Yucatán and the fierce, tropical habanero chile. This recipe has a distinctly Caribbean flair, evoking personal memories of the early market in Merida, capital of the Yucatan and famous for its beaches. There, you'll find wonderful whole fish marinated in achiote paste and cooked on fires on the beach over coconut husks. Or chicken tamales with achiote paste wrapped in banana leaves steamed, then finished over an open fire. These tacos are traditionally served with black beans, rice, and a heaping side of fried plantains (see page 140). You can make your own pickled onions for the garnish: Slice red onions into thin half-moons, sprinkle with oregano, and marinate in the juice from a jar of pickled jalapeños for about 20 minutes.

★ ★ ★

Cut the chicken into ½-inch-wide strips. In a large bowl, mix together the orange juice, oregano, garlic, chile, achiote paste, salt, pepper, allspice, and olive oil to make the marinade. Add the chicken strips to the mixture and let marinate in the refrigerator for at least 1 hour.

To cook the chicken, remove the strips from the marinade and drain off any excess liquid. In a large, heavy skillet, heat the oil over medium-high heat. Sauté the chicken strips, turning once or twice, until thoroughly cooked (cut one to test), about 9 minutes total.

Remove from the heat, squeeze fresh lime juice over the strips, and serve immediately or keep warm in the pan until ready to serve.

To serve, lay the tortillas side by side, open face and overlapping on a platter. Divide the filling equally between the tortillas and top with salsa and pickled onions. Grab, fold, and eat right away. Or build your own taco: lay a tortilla, open face, in one hand. Spoon on some filling, top with salsa and pickled onions, fold, and eat right away.

2 pounds boneless, skinless chicken breasts

½ cup fresh orange juice

2 teaspoons dried Mexican oregano, toasted and ground (page 164)

16 cloves garlic, dry-roasted (page 158)

1 or 2 habanero chiles, dry-roasted (page 154), stemmed, and seeded (use more chiles and/or leave seeds if want more heat)

2 teaspoons achiote paste (page 149)

2 teaspoons kosher salt

1 teaspoon freshly ground black pepper

¼ teaspoon ground allspice

1 tablespoon lemon-infused olive oil (page 162)

2 tablespoons vegetable oil

Lime or orange wedges

8 (5½-inch) soft white corn tortillas (page 13), for serving

Garnish: pickled red onions or orange or pineapple segments

TORTILLAS

Soft white corn tortillas or flautas (page 17)

ACCOMPANIMENTS

Mango-Banana Salsa (page 130),
Tomatillo–Árbol Chile Salsa (page 135)

DRINKS

Margaritas, piña coladas, mojitos

DUCK WITH PECAN PIPIÁN

MAKES 10 TACOS ~ HEAT LEVEL 3
PREP TIME 45 TO 60 MINUTES (PLUS 2 HOURS FOR MARINATING)

Ground nuts or seeds are the singular ingredient in the sauces known as pipiáns, which are sort of like Southwestern pestos. Peanuts, native to South America, were first used, as were pumpkin seeds, but regionally, cooks would incorporate what was available—in the American Southwest, for instance, it could be pine nuts or pecans, or wild hickory nuts in other parts of the country. The richness of the duck is perfectly complemented by this rich, complex sauce that I created to use New Mexico pecans, a wonderful local crop. It's very versatile, a great condiment for grilled satay skewers or as a sandwich spread or a party dip. It's much easier to prepare than it sounds—a whirl in a blender, then a quick turn in a skillet to marry the flavors.

★ ★ ★

To prepare the duck breasts, let the breasts sit on a plate covered with paper towels to absorb any moisture (the breasts need to be dry for the seasonings to stick). In a small bowl, combine the chile powder, salt, and sugar. Sprinkle the seasoning on both sides of the duck breasts and let sit at room temperature for up to 2 hours.

To prepare the sauce, in a large, heavy skillet, heat 2 tablespoons of the oil over medium-high heat and sauté the onion until it begins to caramelize, 5 to 6 minutes; remove from the heat. In the jar of a blender, puree the sautéed onion, the chiles, garlic, tomatoes, canela, sugar, allspice, salt, cumin seed, chipotle puree, and the ½ cup water until smooth.

In the same skillet, heat 3 tablespoons of the oil over high heat until almost smoking. Stir in the sauce and the ground pecans (tilt the pan away from you when you add the sauce as it may spatter) and cook, stirring continuously, until thickened and it coats a wooden spoon well (about the consistency of thick marinara sauce), no more than 2 minutes. The sauce will thicken quickly; do not let it scorch. Remove sauce from the heat and taste to check seasonings. Keep warm until the duck is cooked and all is ready to serve.

To cook the duck, in a cast-iron skillet, heat the remaining 1 tablespoon oil over low to medium heat. Sear the duck breasts, skin side down, until the skin is golden brown and crispy, and all fat has been rendered, about 10 minutes. Turn the breasts

CONTINUED ▶

4 medium boneless duck breasts with skin (about 1¾ pounds total)

1½ teaspoons red chile powder

½ teaspoon kosher salt

½ teaspoon sugar

PECAN-CHILE SAUCE

6 tablespoons vegetable oil

1 small yellow onion, cut into ¼-inch dice

3 dried guajillo chiles, dry-roasted (page 152) and seeded

6 dried ancho chiles, dry-roasted (page 152) and seeded

2 dried cascabel chiles, dry-roasted (page 152) and seeded

7 cloves garlic, dry-roasted (page 158)

5 Roma tomatoes (about 1 pound), blackened (page 164)

1¼ teaspoons ground canela (or ¾ teaspoon ground cinnamon), page 151

1 teaspoon sugar

¾ teaspoon ground allspice

¾ teaspoon kosher salt

¼ teaspoon cumin seed, toasted and ground (page 164)

2 teaspoons chipotle puree (page 153)

TORTILLAS

Soft yellow corn tortillas, crispy yellow corn tortilla shells (page 17), or flautas (page 17)

ACCOMPANIMENTS

Salsa Fresca (page 130), Cascabel Chile–Blackened Tomato Salsa (page 127)

DRINKS

Grenache, light pinot noir

over and cook to medium doneness (145°F), or when the meat retains a line of pink in the center of each breast, about 4 minutes. Remove from the heat, transfer the breasts to a cutting board, and let them sit about 4 minutes. Thinly slice the duck breasts, with skin still attached.

To serve, lay the tortillas side by side, open face and overlapping on a platter. Divide the duck and a generous amount of sauce equally between the tortillas and top with salsa and sprinkle with pine nuts. Grab, fold, and eat right away. Or build your own taco: lay a tortilla, open face, in one hand. Spoon on some filling, top with salsa and pine nuts, and eat right away.

½ cup water

2 cups pecans, ground to a powder

10 (5½-inch) soft yellow corn tortillas (page 13)

Garnish: toasted pine nuts (page 164)

TURKEY WITH MOLE

MAKES 8 TACOS ~ HEAT LEVEL 3 ~ PREP TIME 2 HOURS

Native to North America, turkey has always been a celebratory bird (or at least it was celebrated by those who dined on it). Turkey (*guajolote*, in Spanish) was used for special feasts in pre-Columbian times and was a favorite food of the American Indians. In Mexico today, turkey in mole is still the preferred holiday dish. For Thanksgiving dinner one year at Coyote Café, we raised almost thirty wild turkeys (so much better than the modern domesticated turkey) on open ranchland so they were free to go anywhere and eat anything. The flavor of those turkeys was magnificent! This recipe is a tempting taste of what awaits any traveler to Oaxaca or Puebla, two of the great Mexican mole capitals. Commercially produced mole sauces are widely available throughout most major grocery store chains in the United States. We have used turkey breast for this recipe, but any part of the turkey will work. Note that the turkey must marinate overnight before cooking.

★ ★ ★

In a large bowl, combine the turkey strips and half of the mole sauce. Cover and marinate overnight in the refrigerator.

When ready to cook, drain the turkey strips, reserving the mole marinade. In a large, heavy skillet, heat 2 tablespoons of the oil over medium heat and lightly sear the turkey strips on both sides; set aside.

In a large, heavy saucepot, heat 1 tablespoon of the oil over medium heat. Add the garlic and sauté for 30 seconds (don't let it burn). Add the salt, chicken stock, water, tomatoes, balsamic vinegar, chipotle puree, and raisins and cook for 30 minutes. Remove from the heat. Blend thoroughly and pass through a medium-mesh sieve.

Refry the sauce: In a large, heavy nonstick skillet, heat 1 tablespoon of the oil over high heat until almost smoking. Add the sauce, remove from the heat, and stir to blend. Stir in the Mexican and bittersweet chocolates, and add the sautéed turkey, the reserved mole sauce, and the remaining half jar of mole sauce. Decrease the heat to medium-low and gently simmer, covered, for about 1½ hours, turning the turkey strips every 20 minutes or so. The turkey should be cooked through.

CONTINUED ▶

1¼ pounds boneless, skinless turkey breast, cut into ⅓-inch by 2½-inch strips

1 (8¼-ounce) jar mole sauce, such as Doña Maria

5 tablespoons vegetable oil

6 cloves garlic, dry-roasted (page 158)

1 teaspoon kosher salt

3 cups chicken stock

2 cups water

8 ounces tomatoes, blackened (page 164) and cut into ¼-inch dice

1 tablespoon plus 1 teaspoon balsamic vinegar

1 teaspoon chipotle puree (page 153)

⅓ cup dark raisins (do not use golden raisins)

2 ounces Mexican chocolate (such as Ibarra)

1½ ounces bittersweet chocolate (at least 70 percent cacao)

8 (5½-inch) soft yellow corn tortillas (page 13), for serving

Garnish: toasted sesame seed (page 164)

TORTILLAS

Soft yellow corn tortillas or flautas (page 17)

ACCOMPANIMENT

Mexican Crema (page 160)

DRINKS

Chilled pinot noir or heavy rosé

Remove the turkey from the sauce and set aside. Refry the sauce: In a large, heavy nonstick skillet, heat the remaining 1 tablespoon of oil over high heat until almost smoking. Add the sauce, remove from the heat, and stir to blend. Remove from the heat and pass through a medium-mesh sieve. When the turkey is cool, shred it with your hands and mix with the sauce.

Serve immediately or keep warm in the pan until ready to serve.

To serve, lay the tortillas side by side, open face and overlapping on a platter. Divide the filling equally between the tortillas and top with salsa and sprinkle with sesame seed. Grab, fold, and eat right away. Or build your own taco: lay a tortilla, open face, in one hand. Spoon on some filling, top with salsa and sesame seed, fold, and eat right away.

ESCABECHE TURKEY WITH PICKLED VEGETABLES

MAKES 8 TACOS ~ HEAT LEVEL 5 ~ PREP TIME 40 MINUTES

Before the development of canning, pickling was one of the most important preserving methods, along with salting, drying, and smoking. Particularly in warm countries, pickling was favored for the way it used acid to stop or retard the growth of bacteria. Some historians credit the Egyptians and Romans for developing this technique, which was brought into Spain and then to Mexico. Turkeys, especially ones raised naturally, have a rich, dense flesh and dark, meaty flavor that can stand up to—and are improved by—heartier, more complex flavors like this escabeche. My favorite garnish for each taco serving is a slim feathery frond—no more than two inches long—from the top of a small stalk of fennel. It looks pretty, has good flavor, and is delicious with this filling.

★ ★ ★

Cut the prepared sweet yellow bell pepper into ¼-inch-thick strips (rajas); set aside.

In a large, heavy, nonstick skillet, heat the oil over medium heat. Add the turkey strips and lightly sear on both sides. Add the stock and pickled vegetables (with all their liquid) to the pan and cook until the liquid has reduced to one-fourth of its original volume, about 20 minutes. Transfer the contents of the pan to a large bowl. When the turkey has cooled enough, shred the meat with your hands into long, ¼-inch-wide strips. Discard the remaining liquid and seasonings from the bowl.

To serve, lay the tortillas side by side, open face and overlapping on a platter. Divide the lettuce and filling equally between the tortillas and top with salsa and garnish. Grab, fold, and eat right away. Or build your own taco: lay a tortilla, open face, in one hand. Spoon on some lettuce and filling, top with salsa and garnish, fold, and eat right away.

1 sweet yellow bell pepper, oil-roasted, peeled, cored, and seeded (page 154)

2 tablespoons vegetable oil or olive oil (preferably Spanish)

1¼ pounds boneless, skinless turkey breast, cut into ⅓-inch by 2½-inch strips

2 cups low-sodium chicken stock

Escabeche Vegetables for Turkey (page 158)

8 (5½-inch) soft white corn tortillas (page 13), for serving

Garnish: Iceberg Lettuce Garnish (page 144), chopped fresh cilantro leaves, whole fresh basil or tarragon leaves, or small fennel fronds

---

TORTILLAS	ACCOMPANIMENT	DRINK	55
Soft white corn tortillas	Cascabel Chile–Blackened Tomato Salsa (page 127)	Dry Riesling	

SEAFOOD

CHIPOTLE SHRIMP

58

THAI SHRIMP

59

CALAMARI WITH BLACKENED TOMATO

60

COCTÉL DE MARISCOS

62

DUNGENESS CRAB WITH FENNEL

63

LOBSTER AND AVOCADO

64

CEVICHE WITH COCONUT AND GINGER

66

RED SNAPPER CEVICHE

67

BAJA-STYLE TEMPURA FISH

68

SEARED TUNA

70

SWORDFISH WITH ACHIOTE AND ORANGE

71

MAUI-STYLE SNAPPER

72

CHIPOTLE SHRIMP

MAKES 8 TACOS ~ HEAT LEVEL 7
PREP TIME 15 MINUTES (PLUS 2 HOURS FOR MARINATING)

This combination of sweet shrimp and smoky chipotle has been the absolute favorite at Coyote Café for more than twenty years. The pairing of chipotle and seafood is common throughout Mexico. My most memorable (and outrageous) version was at a party thrown by Patricia Quintana, the famous Mexican chef and writer, for her birthday in her home state of Veracruz. She invited fifty chefs, food writers, restaurant owners, and winemakers to a feast spread out on a river bank where huge pots filled with enormous amounts of crayfish cooked over open wood fires. I must have eaten 200 crayfish, which were cooked with chipotles, roasted garlic, grilled tomatoes, and served with warm tortillas on wood tables and beer trays—and almost disappeared behind a mountain of shells. The shrimp are best when marinated for 1 to 2 hours—any longer is not necessary. For a deliciously smoky flavor, grill the shrimp rather than sautéing them on the stove.

★ ★ ★

In a skillet, heat 2 tablespoons of the oil over medium heat; add the garlic and sauté for 30 seconds (don't let the garlic burn); remove from the heat. In a large bowl, add the shrimp, sautéed garlic, chipotle puree, oregano, and salt. Toss together, cover, and let marinate in the refrigerator for about 2 hours.

In a large, heavy skillet or griddle, heat the remaining 2 tablespoons of the oil over high heat. Decrease the heat to low and sauté the shrimp until they just turn pink and are barely cooked (they will continue to cook after they are removed from the heat). Remove from the heat and serve immediately.

To serve soft tacos, lay the tortillas side by side, open face and overlapping on a platter. Divide the slaw and filling equally between the tortillas and top with salsa and garnish. Grab, fold, and eat right away. Or build your own taco: lay a tortilla, open face, in one hand. Spoon on some slaw and filling, top with salsa and garnish, and eat right away.

4 tablespoons vegetable oil

12 large garlic cloves, minced

1½ pounds small shrimp (40–45 count), peeled and deveined

½ cup chipotle puree (page 153)

1 teaspoon dried Mexican oregano, toasted (page 164)

1 teaspoon fine sea salt

8 (5½-inch) soft yellow corn tortillas (page 13), for serving

Garnish: Baja Cabbage Slaw (page 145), chopped fresh cilantro leaves, chopped onion, grated asadero or Cotija cheese

TORTILLAS

Soft yellow corn tortillas
or crispy yellow corn tortilla shells (page 17)

ACCOMPANIMENTS

Cascabel Chile–Blackened Tomato Salsa
(page 127), Guacamole (page 140)

DRINK

Mexican beer (such as Pacifico)

THAI SHRIMP

MAKES 8 TACOS ~ HEAT LEVEL 5 ~ PREP TIME 30 MINUTES

After Mexican cuisine, Thai is the one that I consider the most expressive. I find its freshness, sharp chile accents, and cool citrus flavors habit-forming, so much so that I travel to Thailand at least four times a year. One of the most distinctive of Thai flavors is that of kaffir lime. It resembles a large key lime with deep green, warty skin and leaves that have a marvelous, haunting perfume unmatched by those of any other lime or lemon. In this filling, I use the leaf to perfume the coconut sauce that cooks the shrimp. The fruit only grows in tropical climates and the lime itself is very hard to find here, but its fresh or frozen leaves are sold at all Asian markets that stock a lot of Thai ingredients. For this filling, the leaves should be minced very finely (remove the rib) or, preferably, ground to a fine powder in a spice mill, as its flavor is so strong that any large bits of leaf will dominate every mouthful.

* * *

In a bowl, combine the kaffir lime, coconut cream, curry paste, sugar, chile, nam pla, and basil. In a large, heavy skillet, add the sauce mixture and the shrimp and bring to a boil slowly over medium heat. Decrease the heat to low and simmer the shrimp until just pink, about 2½ minutes per side. Transfer the sauce and shrimp to a container and let the shrimp cool in the sauce in the refrigerator—about 1 hour. You can prepare the shrimp and sauce up to 1 day ahead, stored airtight in the refrigerator.

To serve, lay the tortillas side by side, open face and overlapping on a platter. Spoon some Thai slaw on each tortilla and top each with 4 shrimp with some coconut sauce. Top with salsa and basil, grab, fold, and eat right away. Or build your own taco: lay a tortilla, open face, in one hand. Spoon on some slaw, then shrimp and sauce, salsa, and basil, and eat right away.

1 kaffir lime leaf, finely minced or ground (about ¼ teaspoon), see headnote

½ cup canned coconut cream or coconut milk

1 teaspoon Thai green curry paste

2 teaspoons sugar

1 red Thai chile, minced

½ teaspoon nam pla (Thai fish sauce)

3 large sprigs Thai basil (about 20 leaves), bruised with the back of a knife to release some of the oils

4 ounces fresh or frozen and thawed Gulf shrimp (26–30 count), peeled and deveined

8 (5½-inch) soft white corn tortillas (page 13), for serving

Garnish: Thai Slaw (page 144) and whole leaves of Thai basil

TORTILLAS	ACCOMPANIMENTS	DRINKS	59
Soft white corn tortillas, crispy white corn tortilla shells (page 17), or 4-inch soft tortillas	Mae Ploy (sweet chili sauce) or Thai barbecue sauce	New Zealand sauvignon blanc, Riesling, mojitos, light beer (such as Asahi)	

CALAMARI WITH BLACKENED TOMATO

MAKES 12 TACOS ~ HEAT LEVEL 4 ~ PREP TIME 40 MINUTES

Along Mexico's Pacific coast, calamari is commonly prepared in homes and restaurants. That area of Mexico was particularly influenced by the so-called Philippine trade routes, where the Spanish ships crossed the Pacific to Acapulco to trade the goods of Asia with the colony. The cuisine has a definite fusion edge—you'll see Asian ingredients like ginger used there, as well as dishes with rice. This recipe comes from the Jalisco region in southern Mexico. It is simpler and more traditional than versions originating from other port cities like Veracruz, the original Spanish port and the area with the most exposure to Spanish influences, including cuisine. The mint is a refreshing and unusual complement to the robust flavor of the blackened tomatoes. The pairing of basil and mint is not traditional, but is one that I like as I think the two herbs work well together.

★ ★ ★

In a skillet, heat the oil over medium-high heat and sauté the diced onion until it begins to caramelize, about 5 minutes. Transfer the onion to a small saucepan and add the calamari, tomato, jalapeño chile, garlic, salt, chile powder, and mint. Let the mixture come to a simmer over medium-low heat and cook until barely done, about 7 minutes (don't overcook or the calamari will be rubbery). Remove from the heat and serve immediately.

To serve, lay the tortillas side by side, open face and overlapping on a platter. Divide the filling equally between the tortillas using a slotted spoon so any excess liquid will remain in the pot and the tortillas won't get soggy. Top with salsa and garnish. Grab, fold, and eat right away.

To build your own taco, lay a tortilla, open face, in one hand. Spoon on some filling, top with salsa and garnish, fold, and eat right away.

¼ cup olive oil (preferably Spanish)

½ small white onion, cut into ¼-inch dice

1½ pounds calamari, cleaned and washed, body sliced into ¼-inch rings and tentacles left whole if small

1 large tomato, blackened (page 164) and cut into ¼-inch dice

1 jalapeño chile, dry-roasted (page 154) and chopped

2 cloves garlic, dry-roasted (page 158) and chopped

¾ teaspoon fine sea salt

3 teaspoons chipotle chile powder (page 151)

1½ tablespoons chopped fresh mint

12 (5½-inch) soft white or yellow corn tortillas (page 13), for serving

Garnish: whole basil leaves, pickled red chile rings

TORTILLAS	ACCOMPANIMENTS	DRINKS
Soft white or yellow corn tortillas	Tomatillo–Blackened Serrano Chile Salsa (page 135), Salsa Fresca (page 130)	Viognier, sauvignon blanc

COCTÉL DE MARISCOS

MAKES 8 TACOS ~ HEAT LEVEL 1 ~ PREP TIME 30 MINUTES

**What Mexicans call a *cóctel de mariscos* is similar to what most Americans think
of as a mixed seafood cocktail. Every port city of Mexico, even inland Mexico
City, offers them (look for a sign advertising *mariscos* or shellfish). Mexico has
some of the freshest seafood in the world, and definitely some of the spiciest. Look
for stands where you can smell the ocean and see the seafood without a blanket of
sauce so you can judge freshness by color and aroma. The classic accompaniment
is crispy tortilla rounds—either chipotle or corn-flavored (usually found next to
the tortilla chips in a Mexican market; saltine crackers are another option). You
need the crunchy texture of the fried tortilla against the softer, juicier texture of
the seafood—so this works great in a crispy taco shell as I've done here.**

★ ★ ★

In the jar of a blender, combine 1 cup of the lime juice, water, chile, cilantro, garlic,
and ⅛ teaspoon sea salt, and puree. Strain through a medium-mesh sieve. Put the
diced snapper in a bowl, pour over the lime-chile marinade, and marinate for 20
minutes.

In a pot of boiling water, add a big pinch of sea salt and blanch the calamari and
scallops for 1 minute. Remove from the heat and scoop out of the water with a slotted
spoon. Cut the calamari into ⅛-inch-thick rings. Cut the scallops into ¼-inch dice.
Set both aside in a bowl.

In a large bowl, stir together the ketchup, Tabasco, Worcestershire, remaining
2 tablespoons lime juice, celery salt, and oil. Drain the snapper well and add to the
ketchup mixture along with the oysters, crabmeat, calamari, scallops, and chives and
toss well to coat with the sauce. The mixture will hold up to 1 day in the refrigerator.
If you make it ahead, prepare the ketchup sauce without the lime juice, which is
added just before serving.

To serve, place some shredded lettuce in each crispy shell, divide the filling
equally between them, top with garnish, and arrange in a taco holder. Or, lean the
filled shells in a row, propped upright, on a platter. Eat right away. To build your own,
place some shredded lettuce, then filling, in a crispy shell, top with garnish, and eat
right away.

1 cup plus 2 tablespoons lime juice

½ cup water

1 serrano chile, stemmed and seeded

4 sprigs of cilantro

1 clove garlic

Fine sea salt

4 ounces boneless, skinless red
snapper fillet, cut into ¼-inch dice

4 ounces calamari

2 large scallops

2 cups ketchup

1 cup Tabasco

1 tablespoon Worcestershire sauce

½ teaspoon celery salt

1 tablespoon olive oil

8 large Pacific oysters, freshly
shucked, with their liquor

4 ounces fresh crabmeat, picked over
for shells

1 tablespoon very thinly sliced
chives

8 (5½-inch) crispy yellow corn
tortilla shells (page 17), for serving

Garnish: shredded iceberg lettuce,
chopped fresh cilantro leaves, lime
wedges, and fine sea salt

TORTILLAS	ACCOMPANIMENT	DRINKS
Crispy yellow corn tortilla shells	A bottled hot sauce (such as Melinda's)	Pineapple Licuado (page 148), Mexican beer (such as Pacifico)

DUNGENESS CRAB WITH FENNEL

MAKES 12 (5½-INCH) TACOS ~ HEAT LEVEL 1
PREP TIME 40 MINUTES

Mexico is blessed with one of the largest coastlines in the world, touching two oceans and two seas. Consequently, it has a very rich and diverse seafood culture. One of the centers for great seafood eating, including crab, is the Atlantic port Veracruz. Seafood vendors populate the market, their counters painted in the hottest tropical colors and the marinated catch of the day displayed in huge sundae glasses. Order *mariscos* of just one type or mix and match—the vendors compete with one another to make bigger cocktails in their own special way. When shopping for fennel, look for ones with tops intact; they add extra freshness to a recipe and a more complete fennel taste. If you cannot find fennel with tops, garnish with one teaspoon chopped fresh tarragon. For extra splash at a more formal party, slices of black truffles (if you want to splurge) or a few drops of truffle oil add elegance.

★ ★ ★

In a large bowl, mix together all of the ingredients except tortillas and garnish and chill in the refrigerator. Serve within 3 to 4 hours.

To serve, lay the tortillas side by side, open face and overlapping on a platter. Divide the filling equally between the tortillas and top with salsa and garnish. Grab, fold, and eat right away. Or build your own taco: lay a tortilla, open face, in one hand. Spoon on some filling, top with salsa and garnish, fold, and eat right away.

8 ounces fresh Dungeness lump crabmeat (avoid frozen), picked over for shells

2 tablespoons lemon-infused olive oil (page 162)

½ cup diced fresh fennel (reserve the feathery tops for garnish)

1 Roma tomato (about 4 ounces), cut into ¼-inch dice

1 large avocado, peeled, pitted, and cut into ¼-inch dice

1 large serrano chile, chopped with seeds

1 tablespoon chopped fresh basil

1 tablespoon chopped fresh cilantro leaves

Pinch of fine sea salt

12 (5½-inch) soft yellow corn tortillas (page 13), for serving

Garnish: chopped fennel tops or pickled jalapeño chile rings

TORTILLAS

Soft yellow corn tortillas
or 4-inch soft yellow corn tortillas

ACCOMPANIMENTS

Salsa Fresca (page 130), Tomatillo-Avocado
Sauce (page 128), or mango-habanero salsa

DRINKS

New Zealand sauvignon blanc
or Mexican beer (such as Pacifico)

63

LOBSTER AND AVOCADO

MAKES 8 TACOS ~ HEAT LEVEL 0
PREP TIME 30 MINUTES (PLUS 1 HOUR FOR MARINATING)

One of the best lunches I've ever had was at the centuries-old Waterside Inn, a Michelin three-star restaurant situated on the banks of the River Thames in Bray, England, and owned by the renowned Roux brothers. Dressed in formal attire, as I was attending the Royal Ascot horse races nearby, I sat down to an unforgettable salad of briny Brittany lobster, rich avocado, tender mâche, sweet mango, and earthy fresh black truffles, all washed down with vintage Krug rosé champagne. I've recreated that memorable combination on many festive occasions and took it as inspiration for these most elegant tacos.

★ ★ ★

Gently toss the lobster, mangoes, lime juice, 3 tablespoons olive oil, and avocados in a large bowl and let marinate for no more than 30 minutes in the refrigerator; lightly season with salt, if necessary. In a bowl, toss the mâche with 2 teaspoons lemon olive oil and a pinch of salt.

To serve, divide the dressed mâche equally between the tortillas, top with lobster filling, garnish with truffle shavings, and arrange in a taco holder. Or, lean the filled shells in a row, propped upright, on a platter. Eat right away. To build your own, place some greens and filling in a tortilla, garnish with truffles, and eat right away.

1 pound cooked lobster meat or cooked large Gulf shrimp (20–26 count) or Dungeness crab

2 ripe mangoes, peeled, pitted, and cut into ¼-inch dice

3 tablespoons fresh lime juice

3 tablespoons plus 2 teaspoons lemon-infused olive oil (page 162)

2 small avocados, peeled, pitted, and cut into ¼-inch dice

Pinch of fine sea salt (optional)

2 cups mâche

8 (5½-inch) soft yellow corn tortillas (page 13), for serving

Garnish: frozen black truffle, thawed and thinly shaved, or black truffle oil (optional)

TORTILLAS

Soft yellow corn tortillas, fried wonton-skin shells (see page 17)

ACCOMPANIMENTS

Tomatillo–Blackened Serrano Chile Salsa (page 135), Salsa Fresca (page 130)

DRINK

Champagne

CEVICHE WITH COCONUT AND GINGER

MAKES 8 TACOS ~ HEAT LEVEL 5 ~ PREP TIME 1 HOUR

The best, most interesting ceviches in the world come from Peru, specifically Lima. Peru is blessed with three completely different geographies—coastal, Amazonian, and highland, with a different ecosystem—and cuisine—for each. Peruvian chefs create ceviches using exotic fish from the coast, potatoes and corn from the highlands, and wonderful tropical flavors and ingredients like hearts of palm from the Amazon region. Typical of a ceviche, the snapper in this taco filling is cooked not with heat, but by chemical action of the acid in the citrus juices. True red snapper, one of the great fishes of the world, is very expensive and rare, distinguished by its large head and red flesh. Most fish that is sold as snapper is actually rock cod or some other rockfish and does not have the subtlety of the genuine article. If you can't get true snapper (you can tell only by seeing the whole fish, with its bright red and pale yellow markings), striped sea bass or halibut will work well. Candied ginger makes a nice garnish.

★ ★ ★

In a large bowl, toss the snapper with the lemon and lime juices and the salt and let marinate for 1 hour in the refrigerator.

Meanwhile, to make the coconut-chile sauce, in a skillet, heat the oil over medium-high heat and sauté the onion just until translucent, 2 to 3 minutes. In the jar of a blender, add the sautéed onion, coconut milk, and chiles and puree until smooth; strain through a fine-mesh sieve into a bowl.

Drain off the marinade from the fish. In a large bowl, toss the snapper with the basil.

Drizzle half of the coconut-chile sauce over the fish and use the remaining sauce as a dip for the tacos. Serve immediately.

To serve, place some iceberg slaw in each crispy shell, divide the filling equally between them, top with garnish, and arrange in a taco holder. Or, lean the filled shells in a row, propped upright, on a platter. Eat right away. To build your own, place some slaw, then filling, in a crispy shell, and eat right away.

1½ pounds boneless, skinless red snapper fillet, cut into ¼-inch dice

½ cup fresh lime juice

½ cup fresh lemon juice

1 teaspoon fine sea salt

1 tablespoon vegetable oil

½ small white onion, cut into ¼-inch dice

¾ cup coconut milk

5 dried ají chiles, seeded and rehydrated (page 152)

2 tablespoons julienned fresh basil

8 (5½-inch) crispy yellow corn tortilla shells (page 17), for serving

Garnish: finely shredded iceberg lettuce tossed with lime juice and a pinch of salt and diced candied ginger

TORTILLAS	ACCOMPANIMENTS	DRINKS
Crispy yellow corn tortilla shells	None	Champagne, pisco sours

RED SNAPPER CEVICHE

MAKES 8 TACOS ~ HEAT LEVEL 8
PREP TIME 30 MINUTES (PLUS 2 HOURS FOR MARINATING)

This is a very basic and traditional ceviche from coastal Peru. There is an ongoing argument in South America about who first invented ceviche, with both the Peruvians and Ecuadorans vying for credit. The Pacific Ocean fisheries that run along the western coasts of these two countries are the most productive in the world. They are the meeting place of some of the greatest deep-sea currents that bring the Arctic waters, full of life, to the surface for feeding the large schools of migratory fish. This recipe is a great way to enjoy the bounty of the sea while still preserving the integrity of the flavors. Try serving these tacos in smaller crispy shells. Guacamole, avocado slices, or diced boiled potatoes are traditional garnishes used to subdue the spicy effect of the chiles.

★ ★ ★

In a large bowl, combine all the ingredients except the tortillas and garnish and let them marinate for at least 2 hours in the refrigerator. Check for salt and serve immediately. The filling can sit for 1 to 2 hours, refrigerated, before it gets mushy.

To serve, divide the filling, salsas, and garnishes equally between the crispy shells and arrange in a taco holder. Or, lean the filled shells in a row, propped upright, on a platter. Eat right away. To build your own, spoon some filling in a crispy shell, top with salsa and garnishes, and eat right away.

2 pounds boneless, skinless red snapper fillets, cut into ¼-inch dice

1 tablespoon habanero hot sauce

¼ cup fresh lime juice

1 tablespoon fresh lemon juice

2 tablespoons olive oil (preferably Spanish)

1 tablespoon fine sea salt

1 tablespoon chopped fresh tarragon

1 tablespoon chopped fresh cilantro leaves

½ red onion, very thinly sliced

1 habanero chile, seeded and minced

8 (5½-inch) crispy yellow corn tortilla shells (page 17), for serving

Garnish: guacamole, avocado slices, sliced boiled potatoes, corn nuts, popcorn

---

TORTILLAS

Crispy yellow corn tortilla shells or 4-inch crispy yellow corn tortilla shells

ACCOMPANIMENTS

Tomatillo-Avocado Sauce (page 128), Roasted Pineapple–Habanero Chile Salsa (page 129)

DRINKS

Coco locos, piña coladas, sauvignon blanc

BAJA-STYLE TEMPURA FISH

MAKES 10 TACOS ~ HEAT LEVEL 1 ~ PREP TIME 40 MINUTES

Batter-fried fish tacos as we know them in the United States originated in the 1930s in Ensenada, Mexico, home to a large Japanese immigrant population who worked in the fishing industry there. Along with their skills as fishermen, the Japanese also brought with them the technique for tempura—deep-frying fish in batter. The Mexicans adapted this technique to make tacos, using young shark, a very inexpensive local catch that held up beautifully when fried. These tacos are best served immediately as fried foods get soggy if left to sit. If you can't find shark, substitute a firm, moist white fish like opah, tilapia, or mahi mahi.

★ ★ ★

To make the marinade, in a large bowl, combine the 1½ cups water, lime juice, garlic, chiles, oregano, and salt. Add the fish strips and let marinate for at least 20 minutes.

To make the tempura batter, in a separate bowl, whisk together the ice water and mustard. Gently stir in the flour, but don't overmix; a few small lumps are okay. Cover and refrigerate for 30 minutes.

Drain the shark pieces and pat them dry with a paper towel.

Have a plate lined with paper towels ready. In a large, heavy-bottomed pot, heat at least 2 to 3 inches of oil over medium heat until it reaches 360°F on a deep-fat thermometer. Remove the batter from the refrigerator and stir once more. Dredge the fish pieces in the batter, a few at a time, to evenly coat. Drop them in the hot fat, 2 pieces at a time, adding 2 more pieces every 30 seconds (fry no more than 4 pieces at a time). Monitor the temperature of the hot oil throughout frying, letting the oil return to proper temperature, if necessary, between batches; to ensure crispness, it must remain a constant 360°F to 380°F. If too low, the fish will be oily; if too hot, the pieces will burn.

Fry them until crisp, light golden brown, and floating in the oil, about 2½ minutes per batch. With a fine-mesh skimmer, transfer the fish tempura to the paper-towel-lined plate to absorb the excess oil. Repeat with the remaining pieces of fish. During frying, be sure to remove any pieces of floating batter, or they will burn and darken the oil, which will transfer a burned flavor to the tempura. Serve immediately.

To serve, lay the tortillas side by side, open face and overlapping on a platter. Divide the slaw and filling equally between the tortillas and top with salsa and garnish. Grab, fold, and eat right away. Or build your own taco: lay a tortilla, open face, in one hand. Spoon on some slaw, then filling, top with salsa, fold, and eat right away.

CHILE-LIME MARINADE

1½ cups water

½ cup fresh lime juice

10 cloves garlic, sliced

2 serrano chiles, stemmed and sliced

2 teaspoons dried Mexican oregano, ground (page 161)

1 tablespoon fine sea salt

2 pounds young shark fillet, cut into 4 by ¾-inch strips (see headnote)

BAJA TEMPURA BATTER

¾ cup plus 1 tablespoon ice water

2½ teaspoons yellow mustard (optional)

1 cup bleached all-purpose flour

Vegetable oil, for deep-frying

10 (5½-inch) soft white corn tortillas (page 13), for serving

Garnish: Baja Cabbage Slaw (page 145), lime wedges, and pickled jalapeño rings

---

TORTILLAS

Soft white corn tortillas

ACCOMPANIMENTS

Salsa Fresca (page 130), Tomatillo-Avocado Sauce (page 128)

DRINKS

Mexican beer (such as Pacifico or Sol), margaritas

SEARED TUNA

MAKES 8 TACOS ~ HEAT LEVEL 3 ~ PREP TIME 40 MINUTES

The tuna for this recipe must be sashimi grade as only the edges will be thoroughly cooked. Sashimi-grade tuna is difficult to find unless you patronize a premium fishmonger or even better, a Japanese fish market, which typically carries it. (If you don't have either in your area, ask at your local sushi bar if they would sell you sashimi tuna. I've bought fish that way.) To be sashimi grade, the tuna not only must be amazingly fresh, but it must be cut from the bottom of the loin, where there is no connective tissue. It should be free of any visible lines (no semicircles within the flesh) or blood, with even color. Its limited supply has made it very costly. The tuna for this filling is quickly seared, a technique known as *tataki* in Japanese cooking. With each mouthful, you enjoy the delicious contrast between the spicy-smoky seared crust of seasonings and the cool raw center of the tuna. Cucumbers add a nice crunch, as does a garnish of colorful sliced radishes.

★ ★ ★

In a large bowl, mix together the red and chipotle chile powders, sea salt, cumin, coriander, oregano, and black pepper. Toss the tuna pieces in the seasoning mix.

In a large, heavy, nonstick skillet, heat the vegetable oil on high heat. Sear the tuna pieces all around, 1 minute per side. Remove from the heat and slice the tuna into ¼-inch-thick slices.

In a bowl, mix the tuna with the cucumber, olive oil, sugar, lemon zest, and salt. Serve immediately. The filling will keep up to 2 hours in the refrigerator.

To serve, place some shredded lettuce in each crispy shell, divide the filling equally between them, top with salsa and garnish, and arrange in a taco holder. Or, lean the filled shells in a row, propped upright, on a platter. Eat right away. To build your own, place some lettuce, then filling, in a crispy shell, top with salsa and garnish, and eat right away.

1 cup red chile powder (page 151)

¼ cup chipotle chile powder (page 151)

¼ cup fine sea salt

¼ cup cumin seed, toasted and ground (page 164)

2 tablespoons coriander seed, toasted and ground (page 164)

2 tablespoons dried Mexican oregano, toasted and ground (page 161)

2 tablespoons black pepper

1¼ pounds sashimi-grade tuna, cut into 2½ by 1½ by 4-inch pieces

1 tablespoon vegetable oil

¾ large English cucumber, peeled, halved lengthwise, and sliced crosswise into ¼-inch-thick half-moons (about 1 cup)

1 tablespoon lemon-infused olive oil (page 162)

¼ teaspoon sugar

1 tablespoon grated lemon zest

¼ teaspoon kosher salt

8 (5½-inch) crispy yellow corn tortilla shells (page 17), for serving

Garnish: Iceberg Lettuce Garnish (page 144) or sliced radishes

TORTILLAS	ACCOMPANIMENT	DRINK
Crispy yellow corn tortilla shells	Roasted Pineapple–Habanero Chile Salsa (page 129)	Pinot noir

SWORDFISH WITH ACHIOTE AND ORANGE

MAKES 8 TACOS ~ HEAT LEVEL 5
PREP TIME 30 MINUTES (PLUS 3 HOURS FOR MARINATING)

An achiote rub is the classic Yucatan way of marinating fish. I tasted this rub for the first time in Isla Mujeres in the early 1970s, when you could still live on the beach in a palapa and hammock, eat great seafood, and drink cold beers for a few dollars per day. The fishermen would rub fish with an achiote-citrus paste and grill them on the beach over fires made from coconut husks. When I worked at Chez Panisse in the late 1970s, I duplicated this rub from my taste memory for some of their famous garlic festivals. The light citrus flavors of the achiote paste are a beautiful contrast to the oily texture of the swordfish. If you don't have swordfish, use another meaty ocean fish such as wahoo or mahi mahi.

★ ★ ★

Mix all the ingredients except for the fish, oil, tortillas, and garnish in a large bowl. Toss the fish cubes in the mixture and marinate for at least 3 hours.

Remove the fish from the marinade, shaking off any excess liquid; discard the marinade. In a large, heavy skillet, heat the oil over medium-high heat and sauté the fish on all sides until cooked through, about 7 minutes.

To serve, lay the tortillas side by side, open face and overlapping on a platter. Divide the shredded lettuce and filling equally between the tortillas and top with salsa and a squeeze of fresh lime. Grab, fold, and eat right away. Or build your own taco: lay a tortilla, open face, in one hand. Add some shredded lettuce, spoon on some filling, and top with salsa and a squeeze of fresh lime. Fold, and eat right away.

½ cup fresh orange juice

2 teaspoons dried Mexican oregano, toasted and ground (page 161)

1½ tablespoons chopped garlic

1 habanero chile, seeded and chopped

3 teaspoons achiote paste (page 149)

2 teaspoons kosher salt

1 teaspoon freshly ground black pepper

¼ teaspoon ground allspice, ground

1 tablespoon lemon-infused olive oil (page 162)

2 tablespoons chopped fresh cilantro leaves

1 Fresno chile, seeded and chopped

1 tablespoon fresh lime juice

1 tablespoon sugar

2 pounds boneless, skinless swordfish fillets, cut into 1-inch cubes

3 tablespoons vegetable oil

8 (5½-inch) soft white corn tortillas (page 13), for serving

Garnish: shredded lettuce and lime wedges

MAUI-STYLE SNAPPER

MAKES 8 TACOS ~ HEAT LEVEL 3 ~ PREP TIME 30 MINUTES

Unlike Baja fish tacos, which are deep-fried in batter, those made Maui-style are grilled. In all my travels, whenever I'm near the ocean—whether it's in Hawaii, Mexico, Alaska, Thailand, or Australia—there has always been a small stand somewhere that serves the local catch in an affordable, portable (usually grilled) form. One of my funniest fish taco experiences occurred in a small town in Alaska where we had stopped for supplies during a sailing trip through Prince William Sound. There in front of us was an old school bus painted in bright, tropical colors now converted to a walk-up kitchen selling, of all things—Maui tacos! We were a long way from Hawaii, but the methods were the same—the local catch (salmon and crab, in this case), simply grilled and served with salsa on fresh tortillas. To reduce the heat of this dish, you can substitute Tabasco for the habanero hot sauce. If necessary, to prevent the pieces of snapper from falling through the grill grate into the fire, use a seafood grilling screen. The pineapple can be grilled ahead, if you prefer, and held at room temperature. Both the pineapple and snapper can also be grilled indoors on a nonstick ridged grill pan. For the pineapple use medium heat, 5 minutes per side; for the fish, very high heat, 3 to 4 minutes per side.

★ ★ ★

Prepare a charcoal or gas grill. In a large bowl, toss the pineapple with the hot sauce. Grill the fruit slices over very low heat until browned and caramelized, 10 minutes per side (don't let the slices blacken or burn). Cut the pineapple rings into small wedges and set aside.

Meanwhile, in a large bowl, combine the oil, lime juice, and salt and marinate the snapper strips in the mixture for 5 minutes (the oil will help prevent the fish from sticking to the grill). Once the pineapple is done, grill the fish over medium-high heat until cooked through, turning once, about 6 minutes total. Remove from the grill and serve immediately.

To serve, lay the tortillas side by side, open face and overlapping on a platter. Divide the lettuce, fish, pineapple, and avocado equally between the tortillas and top with salsa. Grab, fold, and eat right away. Or build your own taco: lay a tortilla, open face, in one hand. Spoon on some lettuce, filling, avocado, and salsa, and eat.

1 small pineapple, peeled, cored, and sliced into rings

¼ cup habanero hot sauce or Tabasco sauce

½ cup vegetable oil

2 tablespoons fresh lime juice

1 tablespoon fine sea salt

1½ pounds boneless, skinless red snapper or mahi mahi fillets, cut into 2½ by ½-inch strips

8 (5½-inch) soft white or yellow corn tortillas (page 13), for serving

Garnish: Iceberg Lettuce Garnish (page 144) and avocado wedges

TORTILLAS
Soft white or yellow corn tortillas or crispy corn tortilla shells (page 17)

ACCOMPANIMENT
Tomatillo–Árbol Chile Salsa (page 135)

DRINKS
Margaritas, coco locos

PORK

TACOS AL PASTOR

MAKES 24 TACOS ~ HEAT LEVEL 3 ~ PREP TIME 1½ HOURS

The meat for these "shepherd's" tacos is commonly seen roasting on vertical spits displayed with pride on street stands throughout Mexico. The spits are usually topped with a pineapple, which is thinly sliced and served in the tacos. This method of cooking meat is identical to that used for the spit-roasted lamb (shawarma) brought to Puebla, Mexico, by Lebanese immigrants in the 1930s. The technique was copied by the Mexican *taqueros* (taco masters), who substituted pork for lamb. The original stand for tacos al pastor still exists in Puebla, with vertical spits of pork still revolving in front of its huge wood-burning hearth. This recipe makes two dozen tacos to serve 8 persons with big appetites, or more as part of a taco party platter. Note that the pork must marinate overnight before cooking.

★ ★ ★

Stem, seed, and rehydrate the dried chiles (page 153). Drain and set aside, reserving the soaking liquid.

In a small saucepan, simmer the orange juice over medium-low heat until reduced by half; set aside. In the jar of a blender, puree the rehydrated chiles until smooth, adding some of the soaking water, if needed, to achieve a smooth consistency.

In a large bowl, add the reduced orange juice, pureed chiles, orange zest, brown sugar, garlic, cumin, oregano, salt, black pepper, vinegar, lime juice, cola, and beer and stir to mix well. Add the pork, cover, and marinate in the refrigerator overnight.

When ready to cook, remove the pork from the marinade and drain well. In a large, heavy skillet, heat the oil over medium-high heat. Sauté the pork pieces until the meat is cooked through, about 7 minutes. Remove from the heat and serve right away or keep warm in the pan until ready to serve.

To serve, lay the tortillas side by side, open face and overlapping on a platter. Divide the filling equally between the tortillas and top with pineapple and salsa. Grab, fold, and eat right away. Or build your own taco: lay a tortilla, open face, in one hand. Spoon on some filling, top with pineapple and salsa, fold, and eat right away.

40 dried guajillo chiles

20 dried ancho chiles

20 dried pasilla negro chiles

2½ cups fresh orange juice

Grated zest of 1 orange

⅓ cup firmly packed dark brown sugar

9 cloves garlic

1½ tablespoons cumin seed, toasted and ground (page 164)

1½ tablespoons dried Mexican oregano, toasted and ground (page 161)

1½ tablespoons kosher salt

1 tablespoon black pepper

1½ tablespoons distilled vinegar

1 tablespoon fresh lime juice

6 ounces cola

8 ounces Mexican beer

4 pounds pork shoulder, cut into ½-inch cubes

3 tablespoons vegetable oil

24 (5½-inch) soft white corn tortillas (page 13), for serving

Garnish: caramelized diced pineapple

TORTILLAS	ACCOMPANIMENT	DRINKS
Soft white corn tortillas	Roasted Pineapple–Habanero Chile Salsa (page 129)	Margaritas made from silver tequila, coco locos, dark beer

PORK CARNITAS

MAKES 8 TACOS ~ HEAT LEVEL 6
PREP TIME 35 MINUTES (PLUS 1 HOUR FOR MARINATING)

In Spanish, *carnitas* means "little meats," and this is probably the most popular taco in Mexican cuisine. The pork pieces are succulent, juicy, and rich with a browned crust from frying—perfect for tacos. The best places in Mexico for this taco are at carnitas restaurants. Every town has one or more, some open only on weekends. You'll see huge cauldrons—thirty gallons or more—of boiling pork fat holding whole pork loins, shoulders, and other big cuts like ribs. The chef closely monitors the frying temperature, pulling out the meat at just the right moment—when cooked, but still juicy. Customers say which cut they want and how much, always getting a mixture of lean and fatty meats, which make better tacos. The meat is weighed and chopped. Once you've paid, you take your carnitas to a table set up with fresh tortillas and bowls of salsa. Order a couple of cold beers and you are in taco heaven. This recipe is much simpler and easier, and the carnitas are great.

★ ★ ★

In a large bowl, add the pork, chile caribe, salt, chipotle powder, and canela. Toss to coat the pork evenly with the seasoning. Let the meat marinate in the spice mixture for at least 1 hour at room temperature.

In a large, heavy skillet (preferably cast-iron), heat the oil over medium heat. Add the seasoned meat and let the pieces sear on all sides. Cook the meat until golden brown and crusty, stirring only occasionally to preserve the crust, about 25 minutes.

Remove from the heat and serve immediately or keep warm in the pan until ready to serve.

To serve, lay the tortillas side by side, open face and overlapping on a platter. Divide the filling equally between the tortillas and top with salsa. Grab, fold, and eat right away. Or build your own taco: lay a tortilla, open face, in one hand. Spoon on some filling, top with salsa, fold, and eat right away.

1½ pounds pork shoulder, cut into ½-inch cubes

1 tablespoon chile caribe (or red pepper flakes), page 151

1½ teaspoons kosher salt

1 teaspoon chipotle chile powder

½ teaspoon ground canela (or ¼ teaspoon ground cinnamon), page 151

3 tablespoons vegetable oil

8 (5½-inch) soft yellow corn tortillas (page 13), for serving

---

TORTILLAS	ACCOMPANIMENTS	DRINKS
Soft yellow corn tortillas, flautas (page 17), or taquitos (page 17)	Tomatillo–Blackened Serrano Chile Salsa (page 135), Green Chile Sauce (page 132)	Pinot noir, sauvignon blanc, ice cold beer

GREEN CHILE PORK MONDONGO

MAKES 8 TACOS ~ HEAT LEVEL 7
PREP TIME I HOUR 20 MINUTES

Mondongo is usually a thick, spicy stew made with beef tripe and lots of locally grown vegetables, probably Spanish in origin. You can find many versions of it throughout Latin America and the Caribbean. The one I am most familiar with was prepared by our wonderful Mexican chef Daniel Alvarez, who cooked at the Coyote Cantina for over twenty years. His version used pork butt instead of tripe, lots of green chiles, sometimes posole or corn, and other green vegetables. He made this dish often for the staff meal and sometimes as a special at the Cantina. It always sold out quickly.

★ ★ ★

Cut the prepared poblano chiles into ¼-inch-thick strips (rajas); set aside.

In a skillet, heat 1 tablespoon of the oil over medium-high heat and sauté the onion until it begins to caramelize, about 5 minutes; set aside.

In a large, heavy nonstick skillet, heat the remaining 2 tablespoons of oil over high heat and sauté the pork cubes until browned, about 15 minutes. Decrease heat to medium-low, add 1 cup of the water, and simmer until tender, about 1 hour, adding 1 cup of the water every 15 minutes after the last cup of water has cooked off so the pan doesn't dry out, until tender, about 1 hour (or more).

Meanwhile, in the jar of a blender, add the reserved chile strips, sautéed onion, garlic, and cilantro and puree until smooth. Season with salt and pepper.

When the pork is tender and all the water in the skillet has dried up, add enough oil to fill the pan bottom about ⅛ inch and heat over high heat until almost smoking. Add the chile puree sauce to the pan with the pork, remove from the heat, and stir to blend. Serve immediately or remove from the heat, cover, and keep warm at room temperature up to 3 to 4 hours. Reheat gently when ready to serve.

To serve, lay the tortillas side by side, open face and overlapping on a platter. Divide the filling equally between the tortillas and top with salsa. Grab, fold, and eat right away. Or build your own taco: lay a tortilla, open face, in one hand. Spoon on some filling, top with salsa, and eat right away.

1 poblano chile, oil-roasted, peeled, cored, and seeded (page 154)

3 tablespoons vegetable oil, plus more for refrying

½ white onion, cut into ¼-inch dice

1¼ pounds pork shoulder, cut into 1-inch cubes

4 cups water

2 serrano chiles, dry-roasted (page 154), stemmed, and seeded

1 garlic clove, dry-roasted (page 158)

Leaves from 1 bunch cilantro

Kosher salt and freshly ground black pepper

8 (5½-inch) soft white corn tortillas (page 13), for serving

Garnish: avocado cubes or strips of roasted poblano or jalapeño chiles

---

TORTILLAS

Soft white corn tortillas (page 13) or flautas (page 17)

ACCOMPANIMENTS

Tomatillo–Árbol Chile Salsa (page 135), Mexican Crema (page 160)

DRINKS

Mexican beer (such as Pacifico), Pineapple Licuado (page 148)

SMOKY BACON

MAKES 6 TACOS ~ HEAT LEVEL 2 ~ PREP TIME 30 MINUTES

Bacon has become a culinary star again, and there are now so many flavors of bacon and ways to enjoy it—traditional smoked bacon, jalapeño bacon, turkey bacon, bacon candy, bacon salt, bacon cocktails, and—the most unusual—bacon ice cream! There are even bacon clubs that deliver different kinds to your door every month. It's the bacon that gives these tacos their flavor. My preference is a natural, nitrate-free, applewood or hickory-smoked bacon that I buy as a slab, rather than presliced, so I can cut strips as I prefer them, about three-eighths inch thick. Most grocery stores and butcher shops sell thick-cut bacon. Also available is center-cut bacon, which is leaner with a higher yield of meat, much like very lean Canadian bacon (which is actually cured pork loin), in extra-thick slices. Wild boar bacon (see Sources, page 167) is particularly tasty for this recipe.

* * *

Have a plate lined with paper towels ready. In a large, heavy skillet, cook the bacon over medium heat until done to your liking. Keep in mind that the bacon will continue to cook for about a minute after it is removed from the pan. Remove the strips from the pan to the prepared plate to drain, leaving the drippings to use to cook the onion. Cut the bacon into 1 by ¼-inch strips and place in a bowl; set aside.

Reheat the bacon fat, if necessary, and sauté the onion over medium-high heat until caramelized, about 5 minutes. Add the sautéed onion to the bacon, along with the honey and red and chipotle chile powders and toss to combine. Season with salt. Serve immediately.

To serve, divide the filling and garnish equally between the crispy shells, top with garnish and salsa, and arrange in a taco holder. Or, lean the filled shells in a row, propped upright, on a platter. Eat right away. To build your own, spoon some filling in a crispy shell, top with garnish and salsa, and eat right away.

12 ounces thick-sliced smoked bacon

½ small white onion, cut into ¼-inch dice

2 tablespoons honey

1 tablespoon pure red chile powder (such as Los Chileros)

½ teaspoon chipotle chile powder

Kosher salt

6 (5½-inch) crispy yellow corn tortilla shells (page 17), for serving

Garnish: tomato slices and shredded radish

TORTILLAS	ACCOMPANIMENTS	DRINKS
Crispy yellow corn tortilla shells, flour tortillas (page 16), or taquitos (page 17)	Cascabel Chile–Blackened Tomato Salsa (page 127), Mexican Crema (page 160)	Merlot, cabernet franc

SONORAN PULLED PORK WITH CHILTEPIN CHILES

MAKES 20 TACOS ~ HEAT LEVEL 5
PREP TIME 6½ HOURS (PLUS TIME FOR MARINATING OVERNIGHT)

The Sonoran landscape is riddled with mesquite trees, wild chile bushes, and barbecue pits. Not surprisingly, the Sonoran people are known for their fiery barbecued meats. Children and grownups alike gather wild chiltepin chiles from the bosque—the forested banks of rivers and streams—and sell them in the markets or next to the serious speed bumps in the road where you must slow down or lose your transmission. This recipe is typical of ranch-style cooking in northern Mexico except that a modern indoor oven replaces the traditional wood-fired barbecue pit. This recipe makes enough for a crowd. To halve, use two and a half pounds bone-out pork butt or four pounds country-style pork ribs, and halve the remaining ingredients, adjusting the cooking time accordingly. Note that the pork must marinate overnight.

* * *

In a bowl, combine the chiltepin and chipotle chile powders, oregano, cumin, canela, coriander, salt, black pepper, and allspice. Rub the dry seasoning mixture on the pork, cover, and marinate overnight in the refrigerator.

Preheat the oven to 300°F. Place the pork in a roasting pan. Mix the water and liquid smoke and add to the pan around the meat. Cover with aluminum foil and bake 3 hours. Remove the foil and bake until the pork is so tender it cuts with a fork, about 2½ hours more.

Remove from the oven and set aside to cool. When the pork has cooled, shred the meat with your hands. Serve immediately.

To serve, lay the tortillas side by side, open face and overlapping on a platter. Divide the slaw and filling equally between the tortillas and top with garnish and salsa. Grab, fold, and eat right away. Or build your own taco: lay a tortilla, open face, in one hand. Spoon on some slaw and filling, top with garnish and salsa, fold, and eat right away.

2 tablespoons chiltepin chile powder (page 151)

1 teaspoon chipotle chile powder (page 151)

2 teaspoons dried Mexican oregano, ground (page 161)

1 teaspoon ground cumin

½ teaspoon ground canela (or ¼ teaspoon ground cinnamon), page 151

½ teaspoon ground coriander

1 tablespoon kosher salt

1 teaspoon freshly ground black pepper

¼ teaspoon ground allspice

1 bone-in pork butt (about 5 pounds)

3 cups water

1 tablespoon liquid smoke

20 (5½-inch) soft yellow corn tortillas (page 13), for serving

Garnish: Baja Cabbage Slaw (page 145), avocado slices, shredded radish

TORTILLAS	ACCOMPANIMENTS	DRINKS
Soft yellow corn tortillas, flautas (page 17), or taquitos (page 17)	Smoky barbecue sauce, Salsa Fresca (page 130), Chipotle Sauce (page 126)	Merlot, California cabernet sauvignon

PORK CHORIZO

MAKES 12 TACOS ~ HEAT LEVEL 6 ~ PREP TIME 30 MINUTES

The chorizo that I've called for in this recipe is the soft, spiced Latin American chorizo made from fresh pork and easier to crumble once out of the casing, not the hard, cured salami-like Spanish kind (although obviously the Spanish tradition was the basis for the Mexican). Chorizo is very easy to make at home if you can't find a good one locally. Use ground pork—preferably ground pork butt, which has the correct proportion of fat to lean. Ask at the butcher shop which cut they use; don't get pork loin, as it is too dry to produce a juicy chorizo. Add good spices and keep the meat moist during cooking by adding water and a little vinegar, and cooking over low to medium heat. Mexican chorizo is available in bulk or links at supermarkets and Hispanic markets and butcher shops.

★ ★ ★

If the chorizo is in links, slit open the casings, remove the filling, and break it up with your hands. Bulk chorizo is ready to use.

In a large, heavy skillet, over medium heat, add the chorizo, cumin, oregano, and black pepper and cook until the sausage renders its fat and is cooked through, about 8 minutes. Remove from the heat and strain off any grease. Mix the cheeses together and sprinkle over the chorizo. Serve immediately or keep warm in the pan until ready to serve.

To serve, lay the tortillas side by side, open face and overlapping on a platter. Divide the filling equally between the tortillas and top with garnish and salsa. Grab, fold, and eat right away. Or build your own taco: lay a tortilla, open face, in one hand. Spoon on some filling, top with garnish and salsa, fold, and eat right away.

1½ pounds Mexican pork chorizo, links or bulk

1 teaspoon ground cumin

¼ teaspoon dried Mexican oregano, ground (page 161)

½ teaspoon freshly ground black pepper

¼ cup grated smoked Cheddar cheese

¾ cup grated asadero cheese (page 151)

12 (5½-inch) soft yellow corn tortillas (page 13), for serving

Garnish: avocado cubes and roasted strips of poblano chiles

PORK CHULETA

MAKES 8 TACOS ~ HEAT LEVEL 0 ~ PREP TIME 15 MINUTES

This is a very simple country-style recipe, kind of like the old family standby of fried pork chops, and is quite tasty if prepared correctly. It is important not to overcook the pork or it will be dry and chewy. In Mexico, pork shoulder chops or other secondary cuts are traditional, but I've used pork loin here to make preparation as easy as possible. Leave any fat on the loin to help keep it moist. If your loin is very lean (and modern pork tends to be very lean), letting it sit in a brine made of 8 cups water, 2 tablespoons kosher salt, ½ cup plus 2 tablespoons sugar, and 1 head garlic, halved, for 2 hours will make the pork juicier and give it a nice aroma.

* * *

In a large bowl, place the pork slices and sprinkle with the coriander, canela, salt, and pepper, being sure to coat the pork evenly. In a large, heavy skillet, heat the oil over medium heat. Add the pork slices and sear on both sides until the meat is barely cooked through, about 6 minutes. Dice the pork into bite-sized pieces and serve immediately.

To serve, lay the tortillas side by side, open face and overlapping on a platter. Divide the filling equally between the tortillas and top with avocado and salsa. Grab, fold, and eat right away. Or build your own taco: lay a tortilla, open face, in one hand. Spoon on some filling, top with avocado and salsa, fold, and eat right away.

1½ pounds boneless pork loin, cut into ½-inch-thick slices

½ teaspoon coriander seed, toasted and ground (page 164)

¼ teaspoon ground canela (or pinch of ground cinnamon), page 151

2 teaspoons kosher salt

½ teaspoon freshly ground black pepper

2 tablespoons vegetable oil

8 (5½-inch) soft yellow corn tortillas (page 13), for serving

Garnish: avocado slices dressed with a squeeze of fresh lime juice

TORTILLAS
Soft yellow corn tortillas or flour tortillas (page 16)

ACCOMPANIMENT
Tomatillo–Árbol Chile Salsa (page 135)

DRINKS
Pinot noir, sauvignon blanc

CHICHARRONES

MAKES 10 TACOS ~ HEAT LEVEL 6 ~ PREP TIME 1 HOUR

A wildly popular Latin snack food throughout the Americas, chicharrones are made from pork belly that has been cooked for a long time with the skin on, and contains a little meat (what we think of as pork rinds in the United States). Though usually eaten as a crispy snack, they also make a tasty taco filling when heated in a sauce until softened and chewy. The most unusual chicharrones are those made from the whole pork skin fried in one piece—they're about four feet long by two feet wide and resemble some dried prehistoric animal. You'll see them for sale on weekends along the highways in areas of Mexico where there are a lot of pigs, sometimes next to a huge pot of pork fat boiling over an open fire. They're almost always made to order; you stop and buy a piece or buy the whole thing. I'm guessing you only see them by the highways because they are so enormous you need a car or pickup truck to get one home.

2 pounds pork belly fat, cut into 1 by 1 by 2-inch pieces

1 tablespoon kosher salt

1½ cups Tomatillo-Blackened Serrano Chile Salsa (page 135)

10 (5½-inch) soft white corn tortillas (page 13), for serving

Garnish: pickled jalapeño rings, chopped fresh cilantro leaves

★ ★ ★

In a large, heavy skillet, add the pork fat and salt and cook over low heat until the pork has fully rendered its fat and the pieces are puffed and airy, about 40 minutes. Transfer the chicharrones to a large saucepan, add the tomatillo salsa, and cook on medium-high heat until the sauce is almost dried up and coats the chicharrones, about 9 minutes.

Remove from the heat and serve immediately, or keep warm in the pan until ready to serve.

To serve, lay the tortillas side by side, open face and overlapping on a platter. Divide the filling equally between the tortillas and top with garnish and salsa. Grab, fold, and eat right away. Or build your own taco: lay a tortilla, open face, in one hand. Spoon on some filling, top with garnish and salsa, fold, and eat right away.

TORTILLAS
Soft white corn tortillas

ACCOMPANIMENT
Green Chile Sauce (page 132)

DRINK
Mexican beer (such as Pacifico)

CARNE ADOVADA

MAKES 8 TACOS ~ HEAT LEVEL 5 ~ PREP TIME 1 HOUR

In the meat section of Mexican markets are large trays of pork or beef sitting in a thick red chile sauce that acts as both tenderizer and flavoring. This is carne adovada. At home, the mixture is slow-cooked into a stew along with additions like posole and vegetables. The chile sauce is a link back to the days before refrigeration, when chiles were used at the market as a preservative. Bueno Foods makes a delicious sauce using New Mexican red chiles that is perfect for this recipe (see Sources, page 167).

★   ★   ★

Preheat the oven to 325°F. In an ovenproof skillet, heat the oil over medium-high heat and sauté the pork pieces until they have a golden sear on all sides, about 5 minutes. Add the chile sauce, cilantro, cumin, canela, and allspice and cover the pan. Transfer the covered pan to the oven and bake until the pork is tender, about 40 minutes, stirring the mixture at least twice during cooking.

Remove from the oven and serve right away with a slotted spoon or keep warm in the pan until ready to serve.

To serve, lay the tortillas side by side, open face and overlapping on a platter. Divide the filling equally between the tortillas and top with garnish and salsa. Grab, fold, and eat right away. Or build your own taco: lay a tortilla, open face, in one hand. Spoon on some filling, top with garnish and salsa, fold, and eat right away.

3 tablespoons vegetable oil

2 pounds pork shoulder, cut into ½-inch cubes

1 (16-ounce) jar Bueno Foods New Mexico Red Chile Sauce (also available frozen in supermarkets in the Southwest), or 2 cups Red Chile Sauce (page 133)

1 tablespoon chopped fresh cilantro leaves

¼ teaspoon cumin seed, toasted and ground (page 164)

¼ teaspoon ground canela (or pinch of ground cinnamon), page 151

¼ teaspoon ground allspice

8 (5½-inch) soft yellow corn tortillas (page 13), for serving

Garnish: toasted pine nuts (page 162), strips of roasted red chiles

---

TORTILLAS	ACCOMPANIMENTS	DRINKS	87
Soft yellow corn tortillas, flautas, or taquitos (page 17)	Tomatillo-Avocado Sauce (page 128), Mexican Crema (page 160)	Dark beer, India pale ale (such as Sierra Nevada), pinot noir, Tempranillo, Malbec	

BEEF, LAMB, AND GAME

SKIRT STEAK FROM ZACATECAS

MAKES 8 TACOS ~ HEAT LEVEL 4
PREP TIME 40 MINUTES (PLUS TIME FOR MARINATING OVERNIGHT)

Skirt steak (*carne de falda*) is a terrific and inexpensive cut for grilling, probably the best for quickly cooked, juicy steaks. For breakfast and lunch all over Mexico, you see them as huge, thin steaks that practically cover the whole plate, but they're really only about six to eight ounces of beef. It's called skirt steak because it's from an area along the outside of the belly of the cow—where a skirt would sit (if cows wore skirts). It's a perfect cut for tacos and fajitas, but be sure to slice against the grain for juicier pieces. The fat on skirt steak is what makes it so tasty, but the meat should not be too fatty—no more than one-quarter covered with a thin layer of fat. Remove any excess. Note that the meat must marinate overnight. You can also cook the meat indoors on a ridged stovetop grill over very high heat, 2 minutes per side.

* * *

Pound the meat with a butcher's mallet until a uniform ¼ inch thick. In a large bowl, combine the garlic, Worcestershire sauce, red wine vinegar, red chile powder, 1 tablespoon of the salt, 2 teaspoons of the pepper, cumin, onion powder, cilantro, oil, and the red and chipotle chile sauces to make a marinade. Rub the mixture over the meat, cover, and marinate overnight in the refrigerator (or less time, if you want more obvious beef flavor).

Prepare a charcoal or gas grill. Season the meat with additional salt and pepper as you throw it on the grill. Grill the meat over medium-high heat, flipping it once during cooking, 6 minutes total. Remove the meat from the heat and cut into ¼-inch-thick strips (my preference) or ¼-inch dice.

To serve, lay the tortillas side by side, open face and overlapping on a platter. Divide the filling equally between the tortillas and top with salsa and garnishes. Grab, fold, and eat right away. Or build your own taco: lay a tortilla, open face, in one hand. Spoon on some filling, top with salsa and garnishes, fold, and eat right away.

1 pound skirt steak, silver skin and most of the fat trimmed away (see headnote)

8 to 10 cloves garlic, dry-roasted (page 158) and chopped

2 tablespoons Worcestershire sauce

2 tablespoons red wine vinegar

1 tablespoon red chile powder

Kosher salt and freshly ground black pepper

1 teaspoon cumin seed, toasted and ground (page 164)

2 teaspoons onion powder

1 tablespoon chopped fresh cilantro leaves

¼ cup corn or other vegetable oil

2 tablespoons Red Chile Sauce (page 133)

1 teaspoon chipotle puree (page 153)

8 (5½-inch) soft yellow corn tortillas (page 13), for serving

Garnish: radishes, lime wedges, finely shredded green cabbage, chopped onions

TORTILLAS	ACCOMPANIMENT	DRINK
Soft yellow corn tortillas	Any salsa from the chapter "Salsas"	Mexican beer (such as Pacifico)

CLASSIC GROUND BEEF WITH GUAJILLO CHILES

MAKES 10 TACOS ~ HEAT LEVEL 4 ~ PREP TIME 40 MINUTES

This favorite of American households is the usual "starter" taco served at schools, airports, and drive-ins, and undoubtedly what most of us picture when we think of tacos. It's the familiar fried folded corn tortilla shell layered with shredded iceberg or romaine lettuce, piquant fresh tomato salsa, and a cumin-flavored ground beef filling topped with grated cheese—but this one is so much tastier. As with any taco served in a crispy shell, fill and eat it right away or it will get soggy. Try to buy a high-quality ground beef, preferably pure ground chuck with a 25 to 30 percent fat content. Less expensive hamburger grinds will work fine, but they won't be as flavorful or juicy.

* * *

In a large, heavy skillet, heat the oil over medium-high heat; add the onion and garlic and sauté until the onion is softened, 3 to 4 minutes. Add the tomatoes, guajillo and serrano chiles, cilantro, cumin, oregano, and the 3 tablespoons of water. Season with salt and pepper. Cook the tomato mixture down until the consistency of a thick marinara sauce. Crumble in the ground beef, mashing and stirring it to combine with the sauce, increase the heat to high and cook, covered, until the meat has lost its pink color and the filling is moist, but not liquid, about 12 minutes. The meat should be soft like meatloaf.

Remove from the heat, stir in the lime juice, and serve right away, or keep warm in the pan until ready to serve.

To serve, divide the lettuce, filling, salsa, and cheese equally between the crispy shells and arrange in a taco holder. Or, lean the filled shells in a row, propped upright, on a platter. Eat right away. To build your own, spoon some lettuce and filling in a crispy shell, top with cheese and salsa, and eat right away.

1 tablespoon vegetable oil

1 small white onion, cut into ¼-inch dice

1 clove garlic, minced

12 ounces tomatoes, seeded and cut into ¼-inch dice

5 dried guajillo chiles, rehydrated (page 152), stemmed, and finely chopped

1 large serrano chile, stemmed and cut into ¼-inch dice

1 teaspoon chopped fresh cilantro leaves

½ teaspoon cumin seed, toasted and ground (page 164)

½ teaspoon dried Mexican oregano, toasted and ground (page 161)

3 tablespoons water

Kosher salt and freshly ground black pepper

1¼ pounds lean ground beef (15 percent fat)

Juice of ½ lime

10 (5½-inch) crispy yellow corn tortilla shells (page 17), for serving

Garnish: Iceberg Lettuce Garnish (page 144) and grated mild Cheddar cheese

TORTILLAS	ACCOMPANIMENT	DRINKS
Crispy yellow corn tortilla shells	Salsa Fresca (page 130)	Cola, dark Mexican beer (such as Negro Modelo)

BEEF RANCHERO

MAKES 8 TACOS ~ HEAT LEVEL 3 ~ PREP TIME 40 MINUTES

The first time I had these tacos was as a teenager on a working ranch owned by family friends outside of Guadalajara. A cadre of cooks from the same family—grandmother, mother, daughter—ran the kitchen. I was fascinated by how they used a comal set over a wood fire to dry-roast the tomatoes. I had never seen tomatoes cooked that way, nor had I ever stood before a live fire in a kitchen, with its bright, dancing flames and the crackling of the wood. The smoky, earthy atmosphere of that kitchen permeated the sauce made with supersweet tomatoes, vibrant onions and garlic, fiery chiles, and aromatic cilantro—so different from any other tomato sauce I'd ever eaten, such a different world of flavors and techniques. That day was one of the transformational moments in my cooking life.

★ ★ ★

Cut the prepared poblano chile into ¼-inch-thick strips (rajas); set aside.

Preheat a large, heavy skillet over high heat. Add the oil to the pan and then quickly add the diced steak and onion. Sauté for 5 minutes, then add the remaining ingredients except for tortillas and garnish. Cook until the meat is cooked and the mixture thickens slightly and is moist, but not wet, about 3 minutes. Remove from the heat and serve immediately or keep warm in the pan until ready to serve.

To serve, lay the tortillas side by side, open face and overlapping on a platter. Divide the filling equally between the tortillas and top with salsa and garnishes. Grab, fold, and eat right away.

Or build your own taco: lay a tortilla, open face, in one hand. Spoon on some filling, top with salsa, fold, and eat right away.

1½ medium poblano chiles, oil-roasted, peeled, cored, and seeded (page 154)

2 tablespoons vegetable oil

1½ pounds strip steak, cut into ¼-inch dice

1 small yellow onion, cut into ¼-inch dice

1 serrano chile, stemmed and minced

3 small tomatoes, blackened (page 164) and chopped

1 teaspoon chopped fresh cilantro leaves

3 cloves garlic, roasted (page 158) and chopped

Juice of 1 lime

½ teaspoon chipotle chile powder

¼ teaspoon cumin seed, toasted and ground (page 164)

½ teaspoon dried Mexican oregano, toasted and ground (page 161)

8 (5½-inch) soft yellow corn tortillas (page 13), for serving

Garnish: grilled cebollitos (charred green onions) sprinkled with salt and fresh lime juice

TORTILLAS

Soft yellow corn tortillas or flautas (page 17)

ACCOMPANIMENTS

Tomatillo-Avocado Sauce (page 128), Tomatillo–Árbol Chile Salsa (page 135)

DRINKS

Margaritas, light Mexican beer (such as Tecate)

STEAMED CARNE SECA

MAKES 8 TACOS ~ HEAT LEVEL 2 ~ PREP TIME 35 MINUTES

This is a very rustic, traditional recipe created for its portability. The charros, the nomadic first cowboys of Mexico and the American Southwest, traveled by horseback far from home so their food was limited to simple choices like jerky that stayed fresh on the trail. You'll find a wide variety of commercially prepared dried beef and buffalo jerky available today, including ones flavored with chiles. Be sure to use an all-natural, preservative-free jerky with consistent color that is fresh and flexible and packaged in an airtight bag. Jerky can be rehydrated directly in boiling water, but most of the flavor will be lost in the water. A tamale steamer or vegetable steamer works well for this process.

12 ounces chile-seasoned beef jerky

8 (5½-inch) crispy yellow corn tortilla shells (page 17), for serving

Garnish: shredded green cabbage, pickled onions (page 146), and lime wedges

★ ★ ★

Place the jerky strips in a steamer or a colander set over gently simmering water. Cover and steam the jerky until very soft and moist, about 20 minutes. Remove from the heat, shred the jerky into long, thin strips along the grain, and serve right away.

To serve, divide the cabbage and filling equally between the crispy shells, top with salsa and garnishes, and arrange in a taco holder. Or, lean the filled shells in a row, propped upright, on a platter. Eat right away. To build your own, spoon some cabbage and filling in a crispy shell, top with salsa and garnishes, and eat right away.

TORTILLAS	ACCOMPANIMENTS	DRINKS	95
Crispy yellow corn tortilla shells, flautas or taquitos (page 17)	Green Chile Sauce (page 132), Cascabel Chile–Blackened Tomato Salsa (page 127)	Mexican beer (such as Pacifico), merlot	

BRAISED BEEF SHORT RIBS

MAKES 8 TACOS ~ HEAT LEVEL 3 ~ PREP TIME 5 HOURS

Be sure to purchase the meatiest short ribs available, without too much fat. They should be thick-cut, 1- or 2-bone size, about 4 inches long, and almost 2½ inches thick. As an interesting alternative to beef, you could try buffalo short ribs. Either way, be sure the meat is fresh and bright red. For the richest, most succulent short ribs, seek out a premium butcher shop where they sell prime beef short ribs, which will have an amazing marbling of fat. Cook over the lowest temperature possible, always below a simmer (you'll see evaporation, but no movement of liquid) until the meat is ultra-tender and falling off the bone. The flavors here are sweet-and-sour Latino, matched well by your favorite dark beer. Caramelized onions make a hearty winter garnish, and very thinly sliced red onions are a fine partner in the summer.

Season the meat evenly on both sides with salt and pepper. In a braising pan with high sides, heat the oil over high heat. Add the ribs to the pan and sear on all sides until browned, about 1 minute per side. Pour in the beer and add the tomatoes to deglaze the pan. Cook, stirring, for 2 minutes. Add the tomato paste, chiles, tamarind paste, garlic, orange zest, brown sugar, canela, bay leaf, allspice, thyme, and beef stock. Decrease the heat to low, cover the pan, and simmer until the meat can easily be pulled from the bone with your fingers, about 4½ hours. Don't overcook the ribs, or the meat will be mushy. Shred the meat and serve immediately or keep warm in the pan until ready to serve.

To serve, lay the tortillas side by side, open face and overlapping on a platter. Divide the filling equally between the tortillas and top with onions and salsa. Grab, fold, and eat right away. Or build your own taco: lay a tortilla, open face, in one hand. Spoon on some filling, top with onions and salsa, fold, and eat right away.

2¼ pounds meaty beef short ribs

Kosher salt and freshly ground black pepper

1 tablespoon vegetable oil

12 ounces dark beer or India pale ale (preferably Sierra Nevada)

5 small tomatoes, blackened (page 164) and chopped

2 tablespoons tomato paste

2 canned chipotle chiles

1 tablespoon tamarind paste (page 164)

3 cloves garlic, dry-roasted (page 158)

2 teaspoons grated orange zest

1½ tablespoons firmly packed dark brown sugar

2 sticks canela (or 1 stick cinnamon)

1 bay leaf

¼ teaspoon ground allspice

Sprig of thyme

4 cups concentrated low-sodium beef stock

8 (5½-inch) soft white corn tortillas (page 13), for serving

Garnish: caramelized white onions or thinly sliced red onions

TORTILLAS

Soft white corn tortillas, flautas or taquitos (page 17)

ACCOMPANIMENT

Mexican Crema (page 160)

DRINK

Dark beer (such as Sierra Nevada)

LA LENGUA

MAKES 14 TACOS ～ HEAT LEVEL 3 ～ PREP TIME 4 HOURS

Tongue—*la lengua*, in Spanish—is a very popular food in Mexico, especially in the central and northern parts of the country, where good grazing land supported a large ranching culture. On ranches, most prime cuts are sold to markets, and the lesser cuts, like tongue, are cooked for the ranch hands. The use of tongue and other secondary cuts of meat, often overlooked, is at the core of peasant cooking. Made rich with brines, marinades, chiles, complex spice mixtures, and rich accompanying sauces, these preparations are some of the most flavorful in all of Latin American cuisine. Tongue is naturally succulent, but needs slow cooking to become really tender and luscious. The flavor is pretty neutral, so this filling has lots of additions to spice it up. A bright salsa is the finishing touch, much like the hot spicy-sweet mustard that was slathered on the tongue sandwiches that I used to eat at my old neighborhood delicatessens.

★ ★ ★

Preheat the oven to 325°F. In a large, heavy, ovenproof braising pan, heat the oil on medium heat. Sauté the onions, carrots, and celery until the onions are just translucent, about 7 minutes. Add all the remaining ingredients except tortillas and garnish, cover tightly with aluminum foil, and place in the oven. Braise the tongue until the meat is very tender and forms cracks in the surface, about 3 hours.

Remove the tongue from the pan, discarding the other ingredients, and allow to cool. Using a paring knife, carefully peel off the skin (which should remove easily); try to leave the tongue intact. Cut the meat into ½-inch-thick slices and cut again into ⅓-inch-thick matchsticks (fine julienne) and place in a bowl. Serve right away or keep warm until ready to serve.

To serve, lay the tortillas side by side, open face and overlapping on a platter. Divide the filling equally between the tortillas and top with garnish and salsa. Grab, fold, and eat right away. Or build your own taco: lay a tortilla, open face, in one hand. Spoon on some filling, top with garnish and salsa, fold, and eat right away.

2 tablespoons vegetable oil

2 medium white onions, cut into ¼-inch dice

2 medium carrots, thinly sliced

2 large stalks celery, thinly sliced

4 cloves garlic, thinly sliced

2 bay leaves

6 cups beef broth

6 dried de árbol chiles, stemmed, seeded, sliced open, and flattened

4 dried guajillo chiles, stemmed, seeded, sliced open, and flattened

2 dried ancho chiles, stemmed, seeded, sliced open, and flattened

2 whole cloves

8 whole allspice berries

2 teaspoons dried Mexican oregano

1 teaspoon cumin seed, toasted and ground (page 164)

1 beef tongue (about 3½ pounds), trimmed

14 (5½-inch) soft yellow corn tortillas (page 13), for serving

Garnish: pickled vegetables, pickled jalapeños, sprigs of fresh cilantro

TORTILLAS	ACCOMPANIMENTS	DRINKS
Soft yellow corn tortillas	Cascabel Chile–Blackened Tomato Salsa (page 127), Chipotle Sauce (page 126)	Tempranillo, Burgundy, Rioja

BARBECUED BRISKET

MAKES 12 TACOS ~ HEAT LEVEL 5
PREP TIME 6 HOURS (PLUS TIME FOR MARINATING OVERNIGHT)

These smoky, wonderfully juicy tacos mix two great culinary traditions—Mexican and Texas barbecue, both notable for their intense, but subtle seasoning. In the United States, the cooking of the Old West was heavily influenced by the charros (Mexican cowboys) who cooked over open fires that infused meat with a smoky essence that so many of us find addictive. In Texas, the wood both of choice and necessity is mesquite, usually mixed with oak to soften the hard green tones of the mesquite. This recipe is easy to do, but requires some advance planning, as the brisket must sit in its rub overnight, and a little patience during the slow cooking. But the results are some of the best tasting barbecue that you have ever eaten. Buy fresh, not prepackaged, brisket that isn't overly fatty—the fat should cover no more than one-third of its surface. Or, you can buy the leaner, thinner end, if you prefer. A piquant cabbage slaw makes a good accompaniment.

* * *

To make the barbecue rub, in a small bowl, combine the smoked salt, ancho chile powder, chipotle powder, and black pepper. Sprinkle the rub over the entire brisket and massage the spices well into the surface of the meat. Place the brisket in a nonreactive pan, cover with plastic wrap, and refrigerate overnight, or at least 4 to 6 hours.

To make the barbecue sauce, in the jar of a blender, add the 2 cups chipotle barbecue sauce, roasted garlic, tomatoes, onion, Tabasco, chipotle puree, and liquid smoke and puree until smooth. You should have about 3½ cups sauce. Reserve 2½ cups for cooking the brisket.

To make a sauce for the tacos, put the remaining 1 cup barbecue sauce in a saucepan with ½ cup water and cook, covered, over low heat, 20 to 30 minutes. Set aside at room temperature if using the same day. Or transfer to a container and refrigerate until needed; gently reheat before serving.

To cook the brisket, in a very large skillet (12 to 14 inches), heat the canola oil over high heat until very hot. Decrease the heat to medium-high and sear the spice-rubbed brisket on both sides, about 2 minutes per side. The spice rub on the meat should be a dark mahogany color, but not burned. Remove from the heat, reserving any browned crusty bits from the pan.

CONTINUED ▶

2½ teaspoons mild smoked salt (preferably Spanish or alder smoked)

1 tablespoon ancho chile powder or mild chile molido powder

1½ teaspoons chipotle powder

1 teaspoon finely ground black pepper

1 beef brisket (about 2½ pounds, 8 by 6 by 2-inch piece)

2 cups smoky chipotle barbecue sauce (or add 2 tablespoons chipotle puree, page 152, to 2 cups of your favorite barbecue sauce)

3 large cloves garlic, dry roasted (page 158)

2 medium Roma tomatoes (about 5 ounces), blackened (page 164)

1 medium white onion, cut into ¼-inch slices, dry-roasted (page 162)

3 tablespoons Tabasco Chipotle Sauce

1½ tablespoons chipotle puree (page 153)

¼ teaspoon liquid smoke

1 tablespoon canola oil

12 (5½-inch) soft yellow corn tortillas (page 13), for serving

Garnish: Baja Cabbage Slaw (page 145)

TORTILLAS	ACCOMPANIMENT	DRINK	99
Soft yellow corn tortillas, or crispy yellow corn tortilla shells, flautas or taquitos (page 17)	Mexican Crema (page 160)	Cold beer (such as Fat Tire)	

Preheat the oven to 275°F. Line a roasting pan with two 18-inch-long sheets of 12-inch-wide heavy-duty aluminum foil. Have another 18 by 12-inch sheet of heavy-duty foil ready. Place 1¼ cups of the reserved barbecue sauce on the foil. On the sauce, place the brisket and any browned, crusty bits from the skillet in the center of the foil. Pour over the remaining 1¼ cups barbecue sauce. Seal into a tight packet by crimping the ends of the foil together and mold the remaining piece of foil around the packet to keep steam from escaping. Place in the oven and cook until you can insert a fork with just a little resistance, about 4½ hours (or about 5 hours if you prefer a more tender brisket).

Remove from the oven, open the foil to let the steam escape (be careful, the steam is hot), and let the meat cool in its juices for about 15 minutes. The meat should pull apart with 2 forks and still have a toothsome texture. Reserve about ½ cup of the meat juices and add to the reserved barbecue sauce and rewarm to serve with the tacos as a sauce.

Shred the meat along the grain with forks and reserve in a saucepan with some of the remaining pan juices. Serve immediately or keep warm in the pan until ready to serve.

To serve, lay the tortillas side by side, open face and overlapping on a platter. Divide the slaw and filling equally between the tortillas and top with crema and barbecue sauce. Grab, fold, and eat right away. Or build your own taco: lay a tortilla, open face, in one hand. Spoon on some slaw and filling, top with crema and barbecue sauce, and eat right away.

GRILLED BEEF WITH PORCINI AND CHILE MORITA

MAKES 8 TACOS ~ HEAT LEVEL 5 ~ PREP TIME 20 MINUTES

The "aha!" moment when I thought to combine porcini and grilled beef with chiles came to me in Argentina, home of the world's best grilled beef. Specifically, I was in Mendoza, the capital of Argentina's wine country and settled by Italian immigrants in the nineteenth century—probably why beef with porcinis is such a common pairing there. This dish is delicious prepared outdoors over a wood-fired grill, but you can also cook it stovetop on a cast-iron griddle or ridged grill pan. Look for porcini powder at specialty food stores or buy dried porcinis and grind them yourself in a spice grinder.

★ ★ ★

If grilling on an outdoor grill, preheat the grill.

In a bowl, combine the porcini powder, smoked salt, and chile powder. Rub over the meat on both sides. Grill the meat over high heat, about 2 minutes per side—you want it really rare and juicy. If cooking indoors on a cast-iron griddle or ridged grill pan, cook, turning once, over very high heat, about 4 minutes total.

Transfer the meat to a cutting board and slice against the grain into ¼-inch strips. To serve, divide the filling equally between the crispy shells, top with garnishes and salsa, and arrange in a taco holder. Or, lean the filled shells in a row, propped upright, on a platter. Eat right away. To build your own, spoon some filling in a crispy shell, top with garnishes and salsa, and eat right away.

1 tablespoon porcini powder (see headnote)

¾ teaspoon smoked salt (page 163)

¼ teaspoon chile powder (preferably morita or chipotle), page 151

1 pound skirt steak, trimmed (no more than one-quarter covered with a thin layer of fat) and pounded ⅓ inch thick

8 (5½-inch) crispy yellow corn tortilla shells (page 17), for serving

Garnish: roasted corn and sautéed porcini mushrooms

TORTILLAS
Crispy yellow corn tortilla shells

ACCOMPANIMENTS
Salsa Fresca (page 130), Chipotle Sauce (page 126), Mexican Crema (page 160)

DRINK
Dark Mexican beer (such as Negro Modelo)

101

CUMIN-SCENTED LAMB LOIN

MAKES 8 TACOS ~ HEAT LEVEL 2
PREP TIME 40 MINUTES (PLUS TIME FOR MARINATING OVERNIGHT)

I lived in Morocco for a time in the mid-1970s studying textiles as part of my anthropology training. While there, I learned to cook with the full array of the expressive, aromatic spices of the Moroccan kitchen. Cumin is one of the most important and widely used of these spices, and I find that its pungent, woodsy aroma gives most meat dishes a "meatier" or "gamier" flavor that I like. Cumin is also widely used in Tex-Mex cooking for the same effect. This brine will work for up to double the amount of meat called for here. When making a brine, use a five-to-one ratio of sugar to salt, which works well for twenty-four-hour brines such as this one. For a North African accent, garnish the tacos with grated carrots, chopped fresh mint leaves, and quartered cherry tomatoes. Look for cinnamon oil in the baking and candy-making sections of well-stocked specialty food stores or online.

★ ★ ★

To prepare the brine, in a large bowl, mix all ingredients except for the tenderloin, oil, tortillas, and garnish. Transfer the brine to a pan large and deep enough to hold the liquid and the meat. Trim the thin outer silver skin from the loin and place it in the brine, cover, and let the meat marinate in the refrigerator for 24 hours. Using your hands, remove the lamb from the marinade, brush off any whole spices from the meat, and pat dry with paper towels.

To cook the lamb, in a large, heavy skillet, heat the oil over medium-high heat. Sear the meat on all sides, turning every 1 to 1½ minutes, cooking to medium-rare (135°F), about 5 minutes total. For lamb loin, sear over medium-high heat 2 minutes per each of the four sides, cooking to medium-rare (135°F), 8 to 12 minutes total. Remove the lamb from the pan and let rest on a cutting board for 3 minutes. Slice the meat into thin medallions and serve immediately.

To serve, lay the tortillas side by side, open face and overlapping on a platter. Divide the filling equally between the tortillas and top with pineapple and salsa. Grab, fold, and eat right away. Or build your own taco: lay a tortilla, open face, in one hand. Spoon on some filling, top with pineapple and salsa, fold, and eat right away.

12 cups water

4 large heads garlic, cloves removed and halved lengthwise

⅔ cup sugar

5 teaspoons kosher salt

4 teaspoons black peppercorns, crushed

14 sticks canela, crushed

4 drops cinnamon oil (see headnote)

4 teaspoons chile caribe (red chile flakes)

2 teaspoons fennel seed, toasted

2 teaspoons anise seed

½ teaspoon ground coriander, toasted

6 drops liquid smoke

1 teaspoon whole allspice, crushed

13 large sprigs flat-leaf parsley

2 tablespoons chipotle puree (page 153)

1 pound lamb loin

1 tablespoon vegetable oil

8 (5½-inch) soft yellow corn tortillas (page 13), for serving

Garnish: caramelized diced pineapple

TORTILLAS
Soft yellow corn tortillas

ACCOMPANIMENTS
Salsa Fresca (page 130),
Mexican Crema (page 160)

DRINK
Tangerine Licuado (page 148)

CHIPOTLE BRAISED LAMB SHANKS

MAKES 10 TACOS ~ HEAT LEVEL 3 ~ PREP TIME 30 MINUTES

The meat from the shank is the tastiest part of the lamb. As lamb is a grazing animal and stands probably 90 percent of the time, the leg muscles get more developed and flavorful. Braised meats take a little more time to cook, but not much time to prepare. They're really very simple and almost foolproof, and the end result is really luscious, flavorful meat. It takes a little longer, but you get the best results if you cook them at as low an oven temperature as possible—around 200°F. Serve these tacos with this richly flavored filling during the colder months, when appetites yearn for something earthy and substantial. Shredding the meat along the grain produces pieces that better retain both moisture and flavor. The meat is best eaten the day it is cooked. Place the meat back in the sauce to reheat.

★ ★ ★

Season the lamb shanks with salt and pepper. In a large, heavy braising pan, heat the oil over high heat. Sear the shanks until browned on each side, 2 minutes per side. Decrease the heat to low. Add all remaining ingredients except tortillas and garnish to the pan, cover, and simmer over low heat until the meat starts to fall off the bones, about 4 hours.

Remove from the heat. Strain the braising liquid and return the strained liquid to the pan. Cook over low heat until thickened and saucelike, about 30 minutes. Shred the meat by hand and return to the pan. Serve immediately or keep warm in the pan until ready to serve.

To serve, lay the tortillas side by side, open face and overlapping on a platter. Divide the filling equally between the tortillas and top with garnish and salsa. Grab, fold, and eat right away. Or build your own taco: lay a tortilla, open face, in one hand. Spoon on some filling, top with garnish and salsa, fold, and eat right away.

2 (14-ounce) bone-in lamb shanks, silver skin trimmed away

Kosher salt and freshly ground black pepper

1 tablespoon vegetable oil

4 cups lamb (or mushroom) stock

½ ounce dried wild mushrooms (such as porcini), rehydrated (page 161)

1 dried pasilla de Oaxaca chile

5 large dried pasilla negro chiles

3 small carrots, cut into ½-inch dice

2 sprigs fresh thyme

½ teaspoon cumin seed

3 garlic cloves, dry-roasted (page 158)

10 (5½-inch) soft white corn tortillas (page 13), for serving

Garnish: sautéed mushrooms, caramelized onions

TORTILLAS	ACCOMPANIMENT	DRINK
Soft white corn tortillas	Mexican Crema (page 160)	Dark Mexican beer (such as Negro Modelo)

ELK TENDERLOIN WITH GREEN CHILE DRY RUB

MAKES 12 TACOS ~ HEAT LEVEL 3–4 ~ PREP TIME 30 MINUTES

A great game meat, elk is more flavorful than deer and not as dry as ostrich. At Coyote Café, elk is a signature dish of chef and partner Eric Destefano, who I say makes the best elk dish in the United States—very juicy and not at all gamy. The trick is to marinate the meat, cook it rare, and let it sit for awhile before slicing. When purchasing elk tenderloin, be sure to have your butcher trim off all the silver skin. If you cannot find elk, axis deer can be substituted (see Sources, page 167). Sautéed wild mushrooms, such as morels, are a nice accompaniment.

★ ★ ★

Preheat the oven to 375°F.

In a small bowl, combine all the spice rub ingredients. Rub the mixture liberally all over the meat. In a large, heavy, ovenproof sauté pan or cast-iron skillet, sear the meat over medium-high heat to caramelize the surface and adhere the dry rub, about 1 minute per side. Remove the pan from the heat and place in the oven. Bake to medium doneness (130°F), about 11 minutes. Remove from the oven, cut into thin slices, and serve immediately or keep warm until ready to serve.

To serve, lay the tortillas side by side, open face and overlapping on a platter. Divide the filling equally between the tortillas and top with garnish and salsa. Grab, fold, and eat right away. Or build your own taco: lay a tortilla, open face, in one hand. Spoon on some filling, top with garnish and salsa, fold, and eat right away.

SPICE RUB

1 tablespoon green chile powder (medium heat), page 151

1 teaspoon smoked salt (page 163)

½ teaspoon kosher salt

½ teaspoon cumin seed, toasted and ground (page 164)

½ teaspoon dried juniper berries, ground (page 159)

¼ teaspoon coriander seed, toasted and ground (page 164)

¼ teaspoon freshly ground black pepper

¼ teaspoon dried Mexican oregano, toasted and ground (page 161)

1½ pounds elk tenderloin, cleaned and trimmed

15 (5½-inch) flour tortillas (page 16), for serving

Garnish: sautéed wild mushrooms (such as chanterelles or morels)

BUFFALO SAUSAGE

MAKES 6 TACOS ~ HEAT LEVEL 4 ~ PREP TIME 30 MINUTES

Buffalo was (and still is) the primary game meat of the American Indians of the Southwest pueblos. They either hunted buffalo or, if they were an agrarian society like most pueblo tribes, they traded corn and other supplies for buffalo jerky and buffalo skins. Orginally, there were over 60 million buffalo or bison roaming the continental United States from the Northwest all the way to Virginia. But by the 1920s, they were almost extinct from overhunting, with only 1,200 left. Fortunately, they have been brought back through effort and careful husbandry, and there are many suppliers of buffalo meat today. When planning my fall menus, I always include buffalo and pair it with local New Mexican fruits like our excellent apples from the Velarde Valley. Any high-quality buffalo sausage will work for this recipe, or substitute a game or lamb sausage.

★ ★ ★

Preheat the oven to 300°F. Cut the prepared green chiles into ¼-inch strips (rajas); set aside.

In a heavy skillet, melt the butter over medium heat. Add the apple slices and sauté until lightly browned on both sides side, about 3 minutes total (be careful not to burn the butter). Transfer to a bowl and set aside.

In a large, heavy skillet, sear the sausages on all sides over medium-high heat until golden brown, about 1½ minutes per side. Transfer the sausages to a baking sheet and bake until cooked through, about 6 minutes.

To serve, cut the links into bite-sized pieces and sprinkle with ground oregano, cumin, and fennel. Combine with the chile rajas and serve immediately or keep warm until ready to serve.

To serve, lay the tortillas side by side, open face and overlapping on a platter. Divide the filling equally between the tortillas and top with crema and goat cheese. Grab, fold, and eat right away. Or build your own taco: lay a tortilla, open face, in one hand. Spoon on some filling, top with crema and goat cheese, fold, and eat right away.

3 medium New Mexico green chiles, oil-roasted, peeled, cored, and seeded (page 154)

2 tablespoons unsalted butter

2 Jonathan apples, peeled, cored, and thinly sliced

9 ounces buffalo sausage

⅛ teaspoon dried Mexican oregano, toasted and ground (page 161)

⅛ teaspoon cumin seed, toasted and ground (page 164)

⅛ teaspoon fennel seed, toasted and ground (page 164)

6 (5½-inch) flour tortillas (page 16), for serving

Garnish: crumbled goat cheese

TORTILLAS	ACCOMPANIMENT	DRINK
Flour tortillas	Mexican Crema (page 160)	Well-oaked chardonnay

RABBIT WITH CHILES AND TOMATILLOS

MAKES 8 TO 10 TACOS ~ HEAT LEVEL 4–5
PREP TIME 45 MINUTES

In Mexico, slow-cooked meats like this are sometimes first wrapped in maguey leaves (from the maguey cactus), which are not available here. In this recipe, the rabbit is braised in aluminum foil with the fresh green aromatics of cilantro and mint, the earthiness of garlic, the tartness of tomatillos, and the heat of jalapeños. The recipe also works well with chicken thighs. Buy the same amount as rabbit and cook as directed here, but remove the skin from the thighs and check sooner for doneness, as they might finish in less time.

★ ★ ★

Dust the rabbit pieces on both sides with salt and green chile powder; set aside.

In a large, heavy nonstick skillet, heat the oil on high heat. Sauté the rabbit until golden, about 2 minutes per side. Remove from the heat, reserving the pan drippings.

Preheat the oven to 250°F. Line a heavy-duty sheet pan or roasting pan with two 24-inch-long sheets of 12-inch-wide heavy-duty aluminum foil. Have another 24 by 12-inch sheet of heavy-duty foil ready. On the foil, place half of the jalapeños, cilantro, mint, garlic, and tomatillos, spreading evenly into a 12 by 12-inch square. Place the sautéed rabbit pieces on the chile mixture and top with the reserved pan drippings. Layer on the remaining jalapeños, cilantro, mint, garlic, and tomatillos. Seal into a tight packet by crimping the ends of the foil together. Mold the remaining piece of foil over the top of the packet. Place in the oven and cook until the meat easily pulls apart and shreds with 2 forks and is still moist without any pinkness.

Remove from the oven, open the foil a little to let the steam escape (use caution, as the steam is hot), and let the meat rest for about 20 minutes. Remove the rabbit from the foil, saving the juices; discard the vegetables.

Shred the meat from the bones and reserve in a saucepan with the pan juices. Serve immediately or keep warm in the pan until ready to serve.

To serve, lay the tortillas side by side, open face and overlapping on a platter. Divide the filling equally between the tortillas and top with garnish and salsa. Grab, fold, and eat right away. Or build your own taco: lay a tortilla, open face, in one hand. Spoon on some filling, top with garnish and salsa, fold, and eat right away.

3½ pound fresh rabbit, cut into 10 pieces (hind legs cut into 2 pieces each)

1¼ teaspoons kosher salt

2 teaspoons green chile powder or jalapeño chile powder (optional)

1½ tablespoons vegetable oil

6 large jalapeño chiles, stemmed and sliced into rings

2 very loosely packed cups fresh cilantro leaves

1 cup very loosely packed fresh mint leaves

6 large cloves garlic, thinly sliced

8 large fresh tomatillos, husked and cut into ¼-inch-thick slices

8 (5½-inch) soft yellow corn tortillas (page 13), for serving

Garnish: sliced red onions and pickled jalapeño chile rings

TORTILLAS
Soft yellow corn tortillas or flautas (page 17)

ACCOMPANIMENT
Tomatillo–Árbol Chile Salsa (page 135)

DRINKS
Pinot noir, Beaujolais, rosé

BREAKFAST

HUEVOS RANCHEROS
112

**HAM AND CHEESE
WITH "BROKEN" OMELET**
113

HUEVOS DIVORCIADOS
114

HUEVOS REVUELTOS
116

**BLACKENED JALAPEÑOS
WITH EGGS AND CHEESE**
117

**BACON AND EGGS
WITH RED CHILE AND HONEY**
118

**POTATOES WITH CHILE RAJAS
AND SCRAMBLED EGGS**
120

**SMOKY YUKON POTATO HASH
WITH PASILLA CHILE RAJAS**
121

**SCRAMBLED EGGS
WITH ROASTED NEW MEXICO GREEN CHILES**
122

HUEVOS RANCHEROS

MAKES 8 TACOS ~ HEAT LEVEL 2 ~ PREP TIME 25 MINUTES

If you are in a rush and don't want to make the Ranchero Sauce, buy a jar of roasted red chile salsa, drain off the liquid, and use what remains. Scramble the eggs over low heat, turning them gently with a wooden spatula or spoon. If the eggs turn white while cooking, the pan is too hot. The chopped cilantro adds bursts of fresh green, herbaceous flavors. For a more robust and traditional finish, squeeze fresh lime juice on the eggs when they are almost finished cooking.

★ ★ ★

In a saucepan, heat the sauce over medium heat; keep warm.

Preheat a large, heavy nonstick skillet over medium-low heat. Melt the butter, then add the eggs immediately after. Cook the eggs until they are done, but not dry, gently stirring and turning them over with a wooden spatula to cook evenly, about 6 minutes. Remove from the pan and serve immediately.

To serve, lay the tortillas side by side, open face and overlapping on a platter. Divide the eggs equally between the tortillas and top each taco with 1 heaping tablespoon of ranchero sauce and your choice of hot sauce. Sprinkle with chopped cilantro. Grab, fold, and eat right away. Or build your own taco: lay a tortilla, open face, in one hand. Spoon on some egg and top with sauces and a sprinkling of cilantro. Fold and eat right away.

1 cup Ranchero Sauce (page 134)

6 tablespoons butter

10 large eggs, whisked together

8 (5½-inch) soft yellow corn tortillas (page 13), for serving

Garnish: chopped fresh cilantro leaves

TORTILLAS

Soft yellow corn tortillas

ACCOMPANIMENTS

Your favorite red chile hot sauce, Tomatillo-Avocado Sauce (page 128)

DRINK

Freshly squeezed orange juice

HAM AND CHEESE WITH "BROKEN" OMELET

MAKES 8 TACOS ~ HEAT LEVEL 1 ~ PREP TIME 25 MINUTES

This is a very simple taco, common throughout Mexico, that I ate at whatever local market was nearby on almost all of my mornings there. It was always accompanied by copious amounts of orange juice freshly squeezed with a portable juicer at a neighboring street cart. They are a great way to start a day and one of my longtime favorites. Consider this recipe a tasty base for ingredients—whatever sounds good to you. Green chile powder is a nice addition, as is chipotle powder.

★ ★ ★

Preheat a large griddle or well-seasoned cast-iron skillet over medium-high heat. Melt the butter and spread it to coat the cooking surface. Crack the eggs on top of each other on the hot griddle. Quickly sprinkle the ham and cheese on top of the eggs and chop the pile a few times with the edge of a wooden spatula. Move the pile around and continue to mix it while it is cooking. Cook the mixture until the eggs are done, but not dry, about 4 minutes. The cheese will brown slightly, but that adds flavor. Remove from the heat and serve immediately.

To serve, lay the tortillas side by side, open face and overlapping on a platter. Divide the eggs equally between the tortillas and top with salsa. Sprinkle with chopped cilantro. Grab, fold, and eat right away. Or build your own taco: lay a tortilla, open face, in one hand. Spoon on some egg and top with salsa and a sprinkle of cilantro. Fold and eat right away.

6 tablespoons unsalted butter

10 large eggs

6 ounces ham, cut into ¼-inch dice (about 1¼ cups)

¾ cup grated Cheddar or jack cheese (about 3 ounces)

8 (5½-inch) soft white corn tortillas (page 13), for serving

Garnish: chopped fresh cilantro leaves

TORTILLAS	ACCOMPANIMENTS	DRINK	
Soft white corn tortillas	Ranchero Sauce (page 134), Green Chile Sauce (page 132)	Freshly squeezed orange juice	113

HUEVOS DIVORCIADOS

MAKES 8 TACOS, SERVES 4 ~ HEAT LEVEL 5
PREP TIME 20 MINUTES

These knife-and-fork (not grab-and-go) egg tacos can be found on almost every breakfast menu in New Mexico and the southwestern United States, and throughout Mexico. They're called *huevos divorciados*—"divorced eggs"—because the eggs are "separated" by their chile sauces, green spooned on one, red on the other. Chorizo or bacon is a nice addition. Two tortillas and two eggs make one serving.

* * *

Heat the red and green chile sauces in separate saucepans and keep warm.

Preheat a large, heavy nonstick skillet to medium-low, melt the butter, then add the eggs and fry sunny side up.

This is a knife and fork taco. For each serving, lay 2 warmed tortillas side by side, open face and overlapping on a plate. Top each tortilla with a fried egg. Spoon some of the red chile sauce around 1 egg, some green chile sauce around the other.

1¼ cups Green Chile Sauce (page 132)

1¼ cups Red Chile Sauce (page 133)

6 tablespoons unsalted butter

8 large eggs

8 (5½-inch) soft yellow corn tortillas (page 13), for serving

Garnish: crumbled cooked bacon

TORTILLAS	ACCOMPANIMENT	DRINK
Soft yellow corn tortillas	Salsa Fresca (page 130)	Freshly squeezed orange juice

HUEVOS REVUELTOS

MAKES 8 TACOS ~ HEAT LEVEL 3 ~ PREP TIME 35 MINUTES

Chorizo was one of the first dishes that I learned to cook at home, prompted by a longing for it after visiting Mexico as a youth, where it was usually served for breakfast with eggs. No more dried, tough, salty bacon for me. I was a chorizo convert, and I was determined to have it for breakfast. While there were good local Mexican markets at the time, I found a simple recipe for chorizo in a Mexican cookbook of my mother's (which I still have almost fifty years later). That homemade chorizo became our Sunday morning ritual. I measured out all the spices—the chile powders, the canela, the cumin, and other seasonings—and added them to the pan along with fresh ground pork. I stirred the mixture slowly, keeping it moist, until it was ready. Breakfast had become exciting again! For this filling, I prefer chorizo that has not been ground too fine and with plenty of fat. You can add additional spices and seasonings like red chile powder or roasted fresh green jalapeños to it while cooking to enhance or alter flavors.

★ ★ ★

If the chorizo is in links, slit open the casings, remove the filling (discard the casings), and break it up with your hands. Bulk sausage is ready to use.

In a small saucepan, add the chorizo and the water, and simmer over medium heat until the chorizo is cooked and all the water is gone (do not let meat get crusty; do not discard fat rendered in the pan), about 6 minutes; do not let the chorizo brown. Set aside and keep warm.

Preheat a large, heavy nonstick skillet over medium-low heat. Melt the butter, then add the eggs immediately after and cook them about 2 minutes. Add the chorizo and any rendered fat to the eggs, remove from the heat, and stir 1 to 2 minutes, until they are done, but not dry.

To serve, lay the tortillas side by side, open face and overlapping on a platter. Divide the egg-chorizo mixture equally between the tortillas and top with salsa. Sprinkle with chopped cilantro. Grab, fold, and eat right away. Or build your own taco: lay a tortilla, open face, in one hand. Spoon on some egg-chorizo mixture, then top with salsa and a sprinkling of cilantro. Fold and eat right away.

12 ounces Mexican pork chorizo, bulk or links

½ cup water

9 tablespoons unsalted butter

8 large eggs, whisked together

8 (5½-inch) soft yellow corn tortillas (page 13), for serving

Garnish: small fresh cilantro leaves

TORTILLAS	ACCOMPANIMENT	DRINKS
Soft yellow corn tortillas	Chipotle Sauce (page 126)	Tangerine Licuado (page 148), light beer (such as Sol or Corona)

BLACKENED JALAPEÑOS WITH EGGS AND CHEESE

MAKES 8 TACOS ~ HEAT LEVEL 6 ~ PREP TIME 1 HOUR

Spicy breakfast foods are the norm in Latin America or Asia, but not in the United States. I have always liked a spicy breakfast, finding that bland, starchy choices like bagels, toast, or pastries with sugar tend to make me sort of sleepy in the morning. This taco filling is another simple version of spicy scrambled eggs and would also make a great omelet when you don't want tacos. Dry-roasting the jalapeños gives the dish a heady, smoky quality and cuts the richness of the eggs. A natural cream cheese would be another tasty accompaniment, with smoked salmon slices for garnish.

★ ★ ★

Preheat a large, heavy skillet over medium-low heat. Melt the butter, then pour in the eggs immediately after. Cook the eggs until they are done, but not dry, gently stirring and turning them over with a wooden spatula to cook evenly, about 6 minutes. Fold in the cheese and chiles during the final minute of cooking. Remove from the heat and eat right away.

To serve, lay the tortillas side by side, open face and overlapping on a platter. Divide the egg mixture equally between the tortillas and top with salsa. Sprinkle with chopped cilantro and a squeeze of lime juice. Grab, fold, and eat right away. Or build your own taco: lay a tortilla, open face, in one hand. Spoon on some egg mixture, then top with salsa, a sprinkling of cilantro, and a squeeze of lime juice. Fold and eat right away.

6 tablespoons unsalted butter

10 large eggs, whisked together

4 ounces grated or shredded jalapeño jack cheese (about 1 cup)

6 jalapeño chiles, stemmed, dry-roasted (page 154), and coarsely chopped

8 (5½-inch) soft yellow corn tortillas (page 13), for serving

Garnish: chopped fresh cilantro leaves, lime wedges

TORTILLAS	ACCOMPANIMENT	DRINK	117
Soft yellow corn tortillas	Tomatillo–Blackened Serrano Chile Salsa (page 135)	Bloody Mary	

BACON AND EGGS WITH RED CHILE AND HONEY

MAKES 8 TACOS ~ HEAT LEVEL 3 ~ PREP TIME 45 MINUTES

Bacon, red chile, and honey are a heavenly combination that I first tried in Santa Fe. I had found a really delectable red chile honey made in the Taos area of northern New Mexico. The combination of sweet, aromatic honey and earthy piquant red chile is a wonderful marriage that enhances both. You can make your own version: add a good fresh red chile powder or puree of fresh red chiles to a wild honey that isn't too sweet. For these tacos, buy the best quality bacon you can find—it will make a huge difference in taste. For a more authentic Mexican flavor, you can substitute guava jam for the honey.

★ ★ ★

Preheat the oven to 325°F. Line a plate with paper towels and have ready.

In a large, heavy skillet, cook the bacon over medium heat until about three-quarters done, about 7 minutes. Add the honey and red chile powder and toss the bacon to evenly coat. Remove from the heat and strain off and reserve any excess honey and bacon grease from the pan. Transfer the bacon to a baking sheet and bake in the oven 5 minutes; remove the bacon to the prepared plate to drain.

Preheat a large, heavy skillet over medium-low heat. Melt the butter, then pour in the eggs immediately after. Cook the eggs until they are done, but not dry, gently stirring and turning them over with a wooden spatula to cook evenly, about 6 minutes.

To serve, lay the tortillas side by side, open face and overlapping on a platter. Divide the egg mixture equally between the tortillas and top with the bacon strips, red pepper or chile strips, salsa, and a sprinkling of cilantro. Or build your own taco: lay a tortilla, open face, in one hand. Spoon on some egg mixture, and top with bacon, pepper or chile strips, salsa, and a sprinkling of cilantro. Fold and eat right away. For a sweeter taco, pour any excess honey and bacon grease over the filling.

10 ounces bacon

5 tablespoons honey

2 tablespoons red chile powder (page 151)

6 tablespoons unsalted butter

9 large eggs, whisked

8 (5½-inch) soft yellow corn tortillas (page 13), for serving

Garnish: strips of roasted sweet red bell peppers or red chiles

TORTILLAS	ACCOMPANIMENT	DRINK
Soft yellow corn tortillas	Tomatillo-Avocado Sauce (page 128)	Freshly squeezed orange juice

POTATOES WITH CHILE RAJAS AND SCRAMBLED EGGS

MAKES 12 TACOS ~ HEAT LEVEL 5 ~ PREP TIME 1 HOUR

These potatoes are buttery, golden, and crisp with a wonderful flavor. Yukon golds are waxy and fry well, finishing with a beautiful golden flesh with browned edges. It's important to pan-fry them in clarified butter and a little vegetable oil, a mix that can withstand the high heat required to get the potatoes crisp and browned without burning.

★ ★ ★

Cut the prepared poblano and serrano chiles into ¼-inch-thick strips (rajas); set aside.

Have a bowl lined with paper towels ready. In a large, heavy-bottomed pot, add 1½ cups of the clarified butter plus the ½ cup vegetable oil and heat over medium-high heat until it reaches 350°F on a deep-fat thermometer. Add the potatoes and fry until golden, stirring them once or twice, about 12 minutes (they will lose about one-third of their volume). The temperature will drop when you add the potatoes; when it returns to 350°F, decrease the heat slightly. Be careful not to burn the potatoes or the oil—the butter-oil mixture should show small, not large, bubbles.

While the potatoes fry, in a skillet, heat the remaining 2 tablespoons clarified butter over low heat and sauté the diced onion until it begins to caramelize, about 10 minutes. When the onion is fully cooked, increase the heat to medium-high and cook a little more to brown the pieces. When the potatoes are done, transfer them to the paper towel–lined bowl to drain off any excess oil. When they are drained, but still hot, transfer to a serving bowl, dust with chile powder and salt, then add the cooked onions and poblano and serrano chile strips and toss to mix all together; keep warm.

Whisk the eggs with 2 tablespoons of the melted butter until the whites and yolks are mixed well. In large, heavy nonstick skillet, add the remaining 2 tablespoons melted butter, pour in the egg mixture, and cook, turning constantly with a spatula, until the eggs are just set, but still very wet, about 2 minutes. Remove from the heat and transfer to a bowl so they don't cook further, cover, and keep warm.

To serve, lay the tortillas side by side, open face and overlapping on a platter. Divide the potato mixture equally between the tortillas and top with scrambled eggs, chopped green onion, and crema. Grab, fold, and eat right away. Or build your own taco: lay a tortilla, open face, in one hand. Spoon on some potatoes and eggs, top with green onion and crema, fold, and eat right away.

3 large poblano chiles, oil-roasted, peeled, cored, and seeded (page 154)

2 serrano chiles, oil-roasted, peeled, cored, and seeded (page 154)

1½ cups plus 2 tablespoons clarified unsalted butter (page 156)

½ cup vegetable oil

1½ pounds small Yukon gold potatoes (with skin), cut into ¼-inch dice

1 white onion, cut into ¼-inch dice

1 teaspoon green chile powder

½ teaspoon kosher salt

12 large eggs

4 tablespoons unsalted butter, melted

12 (5½-inch) soft white corn tortillas (page 13), for serving

Garnish: chopped green onions (green part only) or chopped chives

TORTILLAS	ACCOMPANIMENT	DRINK
Soft white corn tortillas	Mexican Crema (page 160)	Bloody Mary

SMOKY YUKON POTATO HASH WITH PASILLA CHILE RAJAS

MAKES 6 TACOS ~ HEAT LEVEL 8 ~ PREP TIME 30 MINUTES

Tacos are served at all the Mexican markets for workers and shoppers who want a quick bite, including breakfast, as the markets usually open at sunrise. In the Southwest, small restaurants offer whole menus of breakfast tacos (my favorite, Taco Taco, in San Antonio, Texas, offers fifteen morning choices). And breakfast tacos and burritos have become an increasing familiar option along with bagels and pastries at most major airports in the United States and at the drive-throughs of many national fast-food chains. Not only are these vegetarian tacos a fiery morning wake-up, they're good anytime as part of a larger meal, particularly alongside grilled or roasted meats or fish.

* * *

Cut the prepared pasilla and guajillo chiles into ⅛-inch-thick strips (rajas); set aside. In a small skillet, heat the oil over medium-high heat. Add the onion and sauté until it begins to caramelize, about 5 minutes. Remove from the heat and set aside.

In a large pot, add the chile strips, the 7 cups of water, salt, and the potatoes and simmer over medium heat until the potatoes are just tender, 6 to 8 minutes. Transfer the potato-chile mixture to a strainer and let the liquid drain off. Spoon the mixture into a bowl, add the sautéed onion, garlic, chipotle puree, black pepper, and cumin, and stir to blend. Serve immediately or keep warm in the pan until ready to serve.

To serve, divide the filling equally between shells and arrange in a taco holder. Or, lean the filled shells in a row, propped upright. Eat right away. To build your own, spoon some filling into a crispy shell, top with salsa and bacon bits, and eat right away.

2 dried pasilla chiles, stemmed, seeded, dry-roasted, and rehydrated (page 152)

1 dried guajillo chile, stemmed, seeded, dry-roasted, and rehydrated (page 152)

2 tablespoons vegetable oil

1 small white onion, cut into ¼-inch dice

7 cups water

3 tablespoons kosher salt

1 pound small Yukon gold potatoes, cut into ¼-inch dice (with skin)

10 cloves garlic, dry-roasted (page 158)

1 teaspoon chipotle puree (page 153)

½ teaspoon freshly ground black pepper

¼ teaspoon cumin seed, toasted and ground (page 164)

6 (5½-inch) crispy yellow corn tortilla shells (page 17)

Garnish: bacon bits or toasted pine nuts (page 164)

TORTILLAS	ACCOMPANIMENTS	DRINK	121
Crispy corn tortilla shells or soft corn tortillas	Tomatillo-Avocado Sauce (page 128), Guacamole (page 140)	Dark beer (such as Sierra Nevada)	

SCRAMBLED EGGS WITH ROASTED NEW MEXICO GREEN CHILES

MAKES 8 TACOS ~ HEAT LEVEL 3 ~ PREP TIME 40 MINUTES

This recipe highlights the wonderful flavor of the fresh green chiles widely abundant at roadside stands throughout New Mexico during the late summer and all through the fall. Often the chiles are roasted on the spot in hand-turned, butane-fired drums. You can smell the roasting chiles long before you can see them. Just follow your nose to find a vendor, as the air is thick with fiery oils that can clear your head. I look forward to fall in Santa Fe every year mainly because of that nostalgic, pungent and spicy aroma I have come to love.

★ ★ ★

Preheat a large, heavy nonstick skillet over medium-low heat. Melt the butter, then pour in the eggs immediately after. Cook the eggs, gently stirring and turning them over with a wooden spatula to cook evenly, for 3 minutes. Add the chopped chiles, and continue cooking until the eggs are done, but not dry, 1 to 2 minutes more. Remove from the heat and serve immediately.

To serve, lay the tortillas side by side, open face and overlapping on a platter. Divide the egg mixture equally between the tortillas and top with salsa and a squeeze of lime juice. Grab, fold, and eat right away. Or build your own taco: lay a tortilla, open face, in one hand. Spoon on some egg mixture, then top with salsa and a squeeze of lime juice. Fold and eat right away.

6 tablespoons unsalted butter

9 large eggs, whisked together

6 fresh green chiles, oil-roasted, peeled, cored, seeded (page 154), and coarsely chopped

8 (5½-inch) soft yellow corn tortillas (page 13), for serving

Garnish: fresh lime wedges

TORTILLAS	ACCOMPANIMENTS	DRINK
Soft yellow corn tortillas	Salsa Fresca (page 130), Chipotle Sauce (page 126)	Light Mexican beer (such as Tecate)

SALSAS

CHIPOTLE SAUCE

MAKES 4 CUPS ~ HEAT LEVEL 8 ~ PREP TIME 1 HOUR

Why make this versatile sauce yourself instead of buying it already prepared? You'll get a smokier, more interesting result that's free of additives and excess amounts of salt and vinegar of the commercial versions. It's also a great base for other ingredients—tomatillos would be a flavorful addition. Use it in marinades, soups, as part of other sauces, or as a spicy table condiment at a taco party.

★ ★ ★

In a skillet, heat 1 tablespoon of the oil over medium-high heat and sauté the diced onion until it begins to caramelize, about 5 minutes; add the garlic and sauté for 30 seconds (don't let the garlic burn). In the jar of a blender, add the onion, garlic, chiles, brown sugar, salt, tomato paste, vinegar, oregano, and bay leaf and puree until smooth.

To refry the puree, in a large, heavy skillet, heat the remaining 2 tablespoons peanut oil over high heat. Add the puree and bring to a rapid boil, stirring constantly, for 3 minutes. Decrease the heat to medium and cook until the sauce is medium-thick and coats a wooden spoon, about 30 minutes.

3 tablespoons peanut oil

1 small white onion, cut into ¼-inch dice

3 cloves garlic, minced

8 ounces dried chipotle chiles, stemmed and rehydrated (page 152)

¼ cup plus 1 tablespoon packed dark brown sugar

2 teaspoons kosher salt

1 cup tomato paste

½ cup distilled white vinegar

2 teaspoons dried Mexican oregano, toasted (page 161)

1 bay leaf, ground

CASCABEL CHILE—BLACKENED TOMATO SALSA

MAKES 2 CUPS ~ HEAT LEVEL 6 ~ PREP TIME 20 MINUTES

Shake the small, dried medium-hot cascabel chile, and its seeds rattle (in Spanish, *cascabel* **means rattle). Woodsy and smoky, it is a wonderful choice for this richly flavored salsa made with roasted tomatoes and garlic, toasted pumpkin seeds, and caramelized onion. Good with hearty meats from grilled beef to dark-fleshed game like buffalo.**

★ ★ ★

In a skillet, heat 1 tablespoon of the oil over medium-high heat and sauté the diced onion until it begins to caramelize, about 5 minutes. In the jar of a blender, add the onion, tomatoes, cascabel chiles with their soaking water, garlic, pumpkin seeds, and salt and puree until smooth. Strain through a medium-mesh strainer.

To refry, in a large, heavy nonstick skillet, heat the remaining 2 tablespoons oil over high heat until almost smoking. Pour in the puree at once, tilting the pan away from you as the puree will spatter; remove from the heat, stirring to blend. If necessary, refry the puree in batches; you want to refry no more than ½ inch of puree in the pan at one time.

3 tablespoons vegetable oil

½ medium onion, cut into ¼-inch dice

12 ounces tomatoes, blackened (page 164)

12 dried cascabel chiles, dry-roasted (page 152), stemmed, seeded, and rehydrated

2 cloves garlic, dry-roasted (page 158)

5 tablespoons pumpkin seeds, toasted (page 162)

½ teaspoon kosher salt

TOMATILLO-AVOCADO SAUCE

MAKES 4 CUPS ~ HEAT LEVEL 2 ~ PREP TIME 30 MINUTES

The green tomatillo has a bright sharp flavor akin to that of green plums or rhubarbs. In the winter months, when it's sometimes hard to get fresh red tomatoes, I use tomatillos, which are available all year. This sauce makes the ideal cool counterpart to spicy salsas. The unusual addition of ice keeps the cilantro green when pureed with the other ingredients.

★ ★ ★

In a large saucepan, add the tomatillos, onion, cilantro, garlic, chiles, lime juice, salt, and the 4 cups water. Bring to a boil over medium-high heat and boil just until the tomatillos and chiles are blanched, about 5 minutes.

Pour off half of the cooking liquid and add the ice and avocado. Transfer the mixture to the jar of a blender and puree until smooth. Serve this sauce cold. You can prepare it up to 2 days ahead, stored in the refrigerator.

1 pound tomatillos, husked and rinsed

1 small white onion, chopped

Leaves from 1 bunch cilantro

2 cloves garlic

2 serrano chiles, stemmed

2 tablespoons fresh lime juice

1 tablespoon kosher salt

4 cups water

1¼ cups ice

1 large avocado, peeled, pitted, and cut into chunks

ROASTED PINEAPPLE—HABANERO CHILE SALSA

MAKES 3½ CUPS ~ HEAT LEVEL 7 ~ PREP TIME 30 MINUTES

All the vibrant, sun-drenched brilliance of the tropics is captured in this salsa that evolves in your mouth—first sweet, then hot. Luscious ripe pineapple is a perfect partner to the fiery, fragrant habanero chile. Not only is the habanero the hottest chile readily available fresh, when cut open it releases an intense perfume of ripe tropical fruits—mango, pineapple, citrus. As a finishing touch, a squeeze of fresh lime adds a pop of flavor and brightens the sometimes cloying sweetness of a really ripe pineapple. This salsa pairs well with dishes that are tropical in origin or spirit, that have bright, fresh flavors, or that have been simply marinated or grilled, whether fish or meat. It's delicious with almost all fish and seafood tacos and grilled chicken dishes. If you cannot find fresh habaneros, substitute one tablespoon of a fruity hot or extra-hot habanero sauce with a mango base (Melinda's makes a good one) for the habanero chile.

1 pineapple (about 3½ pounds), peeled, cored, and cut into ¼-inch-thick rings

1 orange or red habanero chile, dry-roasted, seeded, and minced (page 154)

1 sweet red bell pepper, cored, seeded, and cut into ⅛-inch dice

1 tablespoon finely chopped fresh cilantro leaves

1 tablespoon fresh lime juice

★ ★ ★

In a large, heavy nonstick dry skillet, cook the pineapple slices (in batches, if necessary) over low heat until caramelized, 6 to 7 minutes per side. (It is important to cook the pineapples on low heat so the sugars in the fruit develop deep flavor, without any burning.) Remove from the heat and cut the pineapple into ⅛-inch dice.

In a large bowl, mix the diced pineapple with the chile, bell pepper, cilantro, and lime juice. Serve immediately for the freshest flavor, but you can make this salsa 1 to 3 hours ahead.

SALSA FRESCA

MAKES 4 CUPS ~ HEAT LEVEL 5 ~ PREP TIME 30 MINUTES

Here is the recipe used at the Coyote Café. Along with chopped onions, fresh cilantro, salsa tomatillo, and red chile sauce, it's always offered as a basic condiment with tacos, regardless of whatever special salsa is paired with a particular taco filling. Salsa fresca is used in Mexico like we use ketchup—to wake up plain foods. But salsa fresca is better than ketchup because it is made fresh—ripe tomatoes, a bit of onion for crunch, the heat of green chile, the tang of fresh lime juice, and the refreshing lift of aromatic cilantro.

* * *

In a large bowl, mix all ingredients together and serve. This salsa is best used the day it's made or the tomatoes become watery.

12 small, ripe Roma tomatoes (about 1½ pounds), cut into ¼-inch dice

2 serrano chiles, seeded and minced

½ small red onion, cut into ⅛-inch dice

Leaves from 1 bunch cilantro, finely chopped

1 tablespoon fresh lime juice

¾ teaspoon kosher salt

¼ teaspoon sugar

MANGO-BANANA SALSA

MAKES 4 CUPS ~ HEAT LEVEL 5 ~ PREP TIME 30 MINUTES

When you want a chile with distinctive flavor and a blast of heat for a salsa with Caribbean roots, the habanero is an obvious choice. It is native to the Caribbean basin, which includes the Yucatán region of Mexico. The flavor of habaneros has tropical overtones that perfectly complement fruit like mangoes and bananas. A little goes a long way—despite its diminutive size, it is the hottest of all chiles available in the United States and Mexico. This salsa makes a great condiment for pork, chicken, or fish.

* * *

In a large bowl, mix all ingredients together. Serve immediately for the freshest flavor, but you can make this salsa 1 to 3 hours ahead.

2 large ripe mangoes, cut into ¼-inch dice (about 2½ cups)

2 medium ripe bananas, cut into ¼-inch dice (about 1 cup)

1 red habanero chile, seeded and minced

1 sweet red bell pepper, cored, seeded, and cut into ⅛-inch dice

Leaves from 1 bunch cilantro, finely chopped

1 small red onion, cut into ⅛-inch dice

1 tablespoon fresh lime juice

Kosher salt

GREEN CHILE SAUCE

MAKES 4 CUPS ~ HEAT LEVEL 6 ~ PREP TIME 1 HOUR 15 MINUTES

"Red or green?" means what color chile sauce do you prefer? It's the usual question posed to anyone ordering a main course in traditional New Mexican restaurants. This is my version of the favorite cooked green chile sauce served with just about everything in New Mexico and other parts of the Southwest. It pairs well with all kinds of dishes, from eggs to roast beef. Make it hot or hotter by the type of chile you use—up to you. I prefer the fall chiles, roasted when they are turning red from green and a little sweeter.

★ ★ ★

In a large, heavy saucepan, heat the vegetable oil over medium-low heat; add the onions and sauté just until translucent, 4 to 5 minutes (do not let them brown). Add the chiles, garlic, and oregano and simmer for 10 minutes, stirring occasionally. Add 2 cups of the water, salt, and sugar and simmer, stirring occasionally, for 30 minutes more. Remove from the heat.

In the jar of a blender, add the chile mixture, lime juice, cilantro, and the remaining ¼ cup water. Puree until smooth.

In large, heavy nonstick skillet, heat the peanut oil over high heat until just smoking. Refry the sauce at a sizzle, stirring constantly, until it coats a wooden spoon, 3 to 5 minutes. Do not allow the sauce to become too thick; add more liquid if necessary. It will keep 1 week in the refrigerator and 1 month in the freezer.

2 tablespoons vegetable oil

2 yellow onions, cut into ½-inch dice

4 cups (about 2⅓ pounds) frozen roasted New Mexican green chile (such as Bueno Foods), page 154, thawed

10 to 12 cloves garlic, roasted and pureed (page 158)

1 tablespoon dried Mexican oregano, toasted (page 161)

2¼ cups water

3 teaspoons kosher salt

1½ tablespoons sugar

1 tablespoon fresh lime juice

1 tablespoon chopped fresh cilantro leaves

2 tablespoons peanut oil or lard

RED CHILE SAUCE

MAKES 4 CUPS ~ HEAT LEVEL 4 ~ PREPARATION TIME 1 HOUR

One herald of fall's cooler weather in northern New Mexico is the ristra—the strings of ripe, red chiles that hang outside to dry alongside doorways and against brown adobe walls. Once dried, the chiles are stored to use throughout the winter in sauces like this one. This recipe is a classic New Mexican red chile sauce and the perfect stage for a whole range of Southwestern foods or as a base for other, more complex sauces from barbecue sauce to moles to stews.

★ ★ ★

In a skillet, heat the oil over medium-high heat and sauté the onion until brown and caramelized, 6 to 8 minutes.

In a blender, add the onion, tomatoes, chiles, garlic, cumin, oregano, and salt. If the reserved chile water is not bitter, add 1 cup of it to the blender; otherwise, add 1 cup plain water. Puree to a fine paste; add a little more chile water or plain water if necessary.

In large, heavy nonstick skillet, heat the peanut oil over high heat until just smoking. Refry the sauce at a sizzle, stirring constantly, until it coats a wooden spoon, 3 to 5 minutes. Do not allow the sauce to become too thick; add more liquid if necessary.

The sauce keeps in the refrigerator for 8 to 10 days; it also freezes well.

1 tablespoon vegetable oil

1 white onion, chopped

8 Roma tomatoes (about 1 pound), blackened (page 164)

8 ounces (about 25) dried New Mexico red chiles, dry-roasted and rehydrated (page 152, soaking water reserved)

2 large cloves garlic, roasted (page 158) and finely chopped

1 teaspoon toasted and finely ground cumin

½ tablespoon dried Mexican oregano, toasted and finely ground (page 161)

1 teaspoon kosher salt

2 tablespoons peanut oil or lard

133

RANCHERO SAUCE

MAKES 4 CUPS ~ HEAT LEVEL 4 ~ PREP TIME 40 MINUTES

This is one of my favorite sauces—it's simple, but often poorly executed. When it's done right—the tomatoes and serranos blackened, the onion and garlic sautéed, the sauce gently fried with some cilantro and roasted poblanos—it's a rustic, vivid, soulful sauce that goes great with eggs, chicken, pork, tamales, and seafood.

★ ★ ★

Cut the prepared poblano chiles into ¼-inch-thick strips (rajas); set aside. Chop together the blackened tomatoes and serranos and set aside. In a large, heavy skillet, heat the oil over low heat and sauté the onion and garlic until soft but not brown, about 10 minutes (add up to ¼ cup water, if necessary, to provide moisture and prevent browning). Add the chopped tomatoes and serranos, two-thirds of the poblanos (reserve one-third of the strips to add at the end), the cilantro, and the salt to the pan. Cover and cook over low heat until the flavors have married and the ingredients have lost their raw taste, 20 to 30 minutes. Remove the cilantro and stir in the reserved poblano strips.

Serve immediately, or hold at room temperature for up to 2 hours. It can be prepared up to 1 day ahead, refrigerated, and gently warmed before serving (don't overcook).

3 poblano chiles, oil-roasted, peeled, cored, and seeded (page 154)

2½ pounds (about 20 small) Roma tomatoes, blackened (page 164)

3 serrano chiles, stemmed and blackened (page 154)

1 tablespoon vegetable oil or lard

1 medium white onion, finely chopped

4 large cloves garlic, finely chopped

½ bunch cilantro, tied with kitchen string

1 teaspoon kosher salt

TOMATILLO–ÁRBOL CHILE SALSA

MAKES 4 CUPS ~ HEAT LEVEL 5 ~ PREP TIME 1 HOUR 10 MINUTES

This sauce is offered at most taco stands throughout Mexico and is probably the one most widely served with tacos. *Chile de árbol*—literally "treelike"—is searingly hot, with a smoky, grassy flavor, but its heat is tamed slightly in this recipe by the tomatoes. A variation using serranos follows.

★ ★ ★

In the jar of a blender, add all the ingredients except for the peanut oil and puree until smooth.

In large, heavy nonstick skillet, heat the peanut oil over high heat until just smoking. Refry the sauce at a sizzle, stirring constantly, until it coats a wooden spoon, 3 to 5 minutes. Do not allow the sauce to become too thick; add a little water if necessary. This sauce will keep for months in the freezer.

Variation: To make Tomatillo–Blackened Serrano Chile Salsa (heat level 7), substitute 5 serrano chiles, dry-roasted (page 154) and minced, for the *chiles de árbol*.

9 tomatillos, husked, rinsed, and blackened (page 164)

6 small Roma tomatoes, blackened (page 164)

10 dried de árbol chiles, stemmed, with seeds

2 cloves garlic

1 tablespoon packed dark brown sugar

2½ tablespoons coarsely chopped fresh cilantro leaves

1 teaspoon cumin seed, toasted and ground (page 164)

1 teaspoon dried Mexican oregano, toasted (page 161)

1 teaspoon kosher salt

1 tablespoon peanut oil

SIDES AND DRINKS

GREEN RICE

MAKES 8 CUPS, TO SERVE 8 ~ HEAT LEVEL 1
PREP TIME 40 MINUTES

This green rice is the side dish that we have used at the Coyote Cantina for over twenty years. Its bright balance of herbs and chiles works well with almost every dish because it is not the usual "red-chile Mexican rice." It tastes of pureed vegetables and chiles, but doesn't overpower some of the milder tacos. And as most tacos contain smoky grilled flavors, this rice provides a fresh accent, rather than duplication of what's already there.

★ ★ ★

Preheat the oven to 400°F.

In the jar of a blender, add all ingredients except for the rice and puree. There should be 5 cups liquid; if not, add more water. Place the chile puree and rice into an ovenproof container and cover tightly with aluminum foil.

Bake until the rice is tender and all liquid has evaporated, about 40 minutes. Mix the rice with a spoon before serving to reincorporate any bits of chopped greens that rise to the top during baking.

Serve immediately. The dish can be made up to 2 hours ahead and held at room temperature. Reheat in a microwave.

Leaves from 1 bunch cilantro

1 poblano chile, oil-roasted, peeled, cored, and seeded (page 154)

1 jalapeño chile, stemmed and seeded

3 green onions, trimmed

2 leaves romaine lettuce

1 tablespoon fresh lime juice

2 tablespoons unsalted butter

3½ cups water

1 clove garlic

1 cup baby spinach

3 teaspoons kosher salt

2¼ cups raw parboiled white rice (such as Uncle Ben's)

RED RICE

MAKES ABOUT 6 CUPS, TO SERVE 6 TO 8 ~ HEAT LEVEL 4
PREP TIME 45 MINUTES

Perhaps expecting the red-tinged, tasteless, so-called Mexican or Spanish rice you see in most restaurants, guests at Coyote Cafe are pleasantly surprised as soon as they take a forkful of this rice. This is a real trailblazer of a side dish, with plenty of personality. For best results, use a good, fresh, pure chile powder. The rice will keep for 2 to 3 days in the refrigerator.

★ ★ ★

In a large, heavy skillet, melt the butter over medium heat and sauté the garlic until soft, 6 to 8 minutes. Stir in the rice. Increase the heat to medium-high. Add the onion, the water, oregano, cumin, marjoram, chile powder, and salt and bring to a boil. Decrease the heat to low, cover, and simmer until the water has just evaporated, 20 to 25 minutes.

Remove from the heat and let stand for 5 minutes. Fluff up with a wooden spoon, adding a little butter, if desired. The rice can be kept warm, covered, in a very low oven or in a rice cooker, and held for up to 2 hours.

4 tablespoons unsalted butter, plus more for finishing

2 cloves garlic, minced

2 cups long-grain rice, rinsed and drained

½ white onion, minced

4½ cups water

1 teaspoon dried Mexican oregano, toasted and ground (page 161)

1 teaspoon cumin seed, toasted and ground (page 164)

1 tablespoon minced fresh marjoram leaves

⅓ cup medium-hot red chile powder

1 teaspoon kosher salt

FRIED PLANTAINS

MAKES 6 SERVINGS ~ HEAT LEVEL 1 ~ PREP TIME 20 MINUTES

Plantains are cooked at all stages of ripeness, but for this recipe, they should be bought and used green for ease in slicing and frying. These chips are great for buffets and go well with with tacos with seafood fillings.

★ ★ ★

Line a plate with paper towels and have ready. In a small bowl, combine the salt, chile powder, canela, and allspice; set aside. In a large, heavy pot, heat the oil over medium heat until it reaches 350°F on a deep-fat thermometer.

Peel the plantains with a paring knife. With a mandoline or hand-held vegetable slicer, cut them lengthwise into paper-thin strips. Fry the plantains in batches, flipping them in the oil, until crisp and light brown, 30 seconds to 1 minute per batch. Remove with a slotted spoon to the prepared plate to drain.

Transfer to a large bowl and toss with chile seasoning while still warm. The chips will keep stored airtight in a cool, dry place for 1 day.

½ teaspoon kosher salt

½ teaspoon red chile powder (page 151)

½ teaspoon ground canela (or ¼ teaspoon ground cinnamon), page 151

⅛ teaspoon ground Jamaican allspice

8 cups vegetable oil, for deep-frying

2½ pounds large green plantains

GUACAMOLE

MAKES 3½ CUPS ~ HEAT LEVEL 5 ~ PREP TIME 15 MINUTES

Guacamole means "sauce made with avocado" and comes from Nahuatl, the pre-Columbian language still spoken in some parts of Mexico: *guac*—avocado—and *mole*—a sauce made of more than one chile or ingredient. The best guacamoles are prepared in a stone mortar or *molcajete*. The chiles and cilantro are ground with lime and salt, and the avocados and tomatoes are mashed in, layering the flavors and creating a coarser, more interesting texture.

★ ★ ★

Place the avocados, tomatoes, cilantro, onion, and lime juice in a bowl and gently mash with a fork to blend together. Slowly add the salt and chiles, mixing and tasting until seasoned to your liking. Serve immediately.

4 medium avocados

2 Roma tomatoes

3 tablespoons chopped cilantro

1 teaspoon chopped red onion, rinsed briefly under cold water

1½ tablespoons fresh lime juice

1¼ teaspoons kosher salt

4 large serrano chiles, stemmed and minced very fine, with seeds

CHARRO BEANS

MAKES 8 CUPS, TO SERVE 8 ~ HEAT LEVEL 2
PREP TIME 30 MINUTES (PLUS 4 HOURS FOR COOKING)

Here is another great side dish for tacos. The beans have a smoky taste from the bacon and smoked salt that makes them a particularly good match for meaty, northern-style dishes featuring beef, lamb, or pork. These pintos are spicier than black beans because of the jalapeños, and you don't need to cook them as long—just until they are soft. Serve them in bowls with their juices—a perfect addition to any barbecue menu. They're also hearty enough to be served alone as a meal. (Photo page 137.)

★ ★ ★

To cook the pinto beans, place the onions, garlic, and bay leaf in cheesecloth and tie into a pouch. In a large soup pot, place the pouch, beans, and water and bring to a boil over high heat. Decrease the heat to medium-low, and gently boil until the beans are soft, but not disintegrating, about 4 hours. Discard the seasoning pouch. Stir in the kosher and smoked salts. The beans can be prepared ahead and reheated, if desired.

To prepare the meat mixture, if the chorizo is in links, slit open the casings, remove the filling, and break it up with your hands. Bulk sausage is ready to use. Set aside.

In a large, heavy skillet, sauté the bacon, onion, garlic, and chorizo over medium-high heat for 5 minutes, stirring occasionally so the garlic doesn't burn. Add the jalapeños, tomato, and ham and cook 2 minutes more.

To serve, add the meat mixture to the beans and garnish with chopped fresh cilantro and lime wedges.

PINTO BEANS

2 white onions, cut into ½-inch dice

1 clove garlic

1 bay leaf

3 cups dried pinto beans, rinsed 3 times and picked over for rocks

14 cups water

½ teaspoon kosher salt

½ teaspoon smoked salt (page 163)

MEAT

6 ounces Mexican pork chorizo, bulk or links

¾ cup diced bacon

1 small white onion, cut in ¼-inch dice

2 cloves garlic, minced

½ cup chopped canned pickled jalapeño chiles, drained (page 154)

1 large fresh tomato, seeded and chopped (about ¾ cup)

½ cup diced ham

Garnish: chopped fresh cilantro leaves, lime wedges

TRADITIONAL REFRITOS

MAKES 8 LARGE SERVINGS ~ HEAT LEVEL 5 ~ PREP TIME 45 MINUTES
(PLUS 12 HOURS SOAKING TIME AND 6 HOURS COOKING TIME)

Refritos—refried beans—are one of the most common side dishes in Mexican and Southwestern restaurants. Finding a good rendition, though, is rare. Most places use flavorless canned beans for a base—already a poor start. And they don't take the time to slowly cook and stir them to infuse the mixture with flavor and texture. The best refritos are made from beans cooked from scratch with many different seasonings so the beans absorb the flavors and the cooking liquid is intense and balanced. Here are two recipes for refritos. The first is for black beans cooked from a dried state, which takes several hours to prepare. The second requires just forty minutes and uses canned black beans that are already cooked as a base.

★ ★ ★

Drain the beans, watching for any rocks you might have missed earlier, and place in a large, heavy pot. Add the water, garlic, onion, chipotle puree, tomato paste, thyme, bay leaf, cumin, tomatoes, and chile, and gently simmer over low to medium heat, stirring occasionally, until the beans are tender, about 2½ hours. Add small amounts of water as necessary to keep the beans covered, but not more than you need or the beans will be watery.

When cooked, remove from the heat and add the salt. Remove the bay leaf and garlic. Squeeze out the softened garlic cloves from their skins back and return to the pot. In the jar of a blender, add the contents of the pot and puree until smooth.

To refry the bean puree, in a large, heavy nonstick skillet, heat the oil over high heat. Add the puree and bring to a rapid boil, stirring constantly, for 3 minutes. Decrease the heat to medium-high and cook until the beans are a thick, semisolid consistency, about 20 minutes. Adjust the salt, if necessary.

8 ounces dried black beans, rinsed 2 or 3 times in cold water and picked over for stones

4 quarts plus 1 cup (more or less) water

1 head garlic, halved

½ large white onion

3 teaspoons chipotle puree (page 153)

3 teaspoons tomato paste

¼ teaspoon dried thyme

1 bay leaf

¼ teaspoon cumin seed, toasted and ground (page 164)

3 small Roma tomatoes, blackened (page 164), or fire-roasted canned tomatoes, if available

1 jalapeño chile, dry-roasted and stemmed

1 tablespoon kosher salt

¼ cup vegetable oil, for refrying

QUICK REFRITOS

MAKES 6 SERVINGS ~ HEAT LEVEL 4 ~ PREP TIME 40 MINUTES

If you don't have time to cook your beans for refritos, for a better base, buy a Mexican brand of canned black beans like La Casteño, which have more flavor, or the Ranch brand, which have been cooked with jalapeños.

★ ★ ★

In a saucepan, add the beans, garlic, tomatoes, chipotle puree, cumin seed, and salt and bring to a boil over medium-high heat. Remove from the heat. In the jar of a blender, add the bean mixture and puree until very smooth.

To refry the bean puree, in a large, heavy nonstick skillet, heat the oil over medium-high heat. Add the puree and bring to a rapid boil, stirring constantly, until no steam rises from the beans and the liquid is evaporated. Decrease the heat to medium and cook, stirring constantly, until the beans are a thick, semisolid consistency and slightly crusted and browned, about 20 minutes. Stir in the cilantro and adjust the salt, if necessary. Note: If you want the beans extra-spicy and smoky, add up to 4 more tablespoons chipotle puree. For the most authentic refritos, substitute 3 tablespoons pork lard or duck fat for the vegetable oil.

2 (20-ounce) cans black beans (preferably a Mexican brand such as La Casteña), with liquid

10 cloves garlic, roasted (page 158)

4 Roma tomatoes, blackened (page 164)

2 tablespoons chipotle puree (page 153)

¼ teaspoon cumin seed, toasted and ground (page 164)

Kosher salt

3 tablespoons vegetable oil, for refrying

2 tablespoons coarsely chopped fresh cilantro leaves

THAI SLAW

MAKES ABOUT 2 CUPS ~ HEAT LEVEL 6 ~ PREP TIME 10 MINUTES

One of the preparations that make Thai cuisine so fresh and refreshing in the tropical heat is its raw vegetable salads that serve as backdrops to fish or meat. The sauce used on these salads is typically a blend of chiles, fish sauce, fresh lime juice, and herbs, with fresh cabbage as one of the side dishes. This Thai slaw is inspired by those classic recipes. Use it as a base for Thai Shrimp tacos (page 59) or for other shrimp or seafood fillings.

★ ★ ★

In a bowl, combine all ingredients. Use within 1 to 2 hours.

2 cups very thinly sliced Napa cabbage (leaves only, ribs trimmed away)

1 minced Thai chile

½ teaspoon unseasoned rice wine vinegar

½ teaspoon fresh lime juice

¼ teaspoon kosher salt

A few drops nam pla (Thai fish sauce), optional

1 tablespoon chopped Thai basil

1 tablespoon coarsely chopped fresh cilantro

ICEBERG LETTUCE GARNISH

MAKES 3 CUPS, ENOUGH FOR 12 TACOS ~ HEAT LEVEL 4
PREP TIME 15 MINUTES

This is the classic vegetable layer for the familiar ground beef taco. It adds freshness and crunch to the taco and absorbs some of the meat juices, but you can use it with any number of other fillings—up to you. The addition of salsa fresca to bland iceberg lettuce adds vibrant color and flavor.

★ ★ ★

Line a bowl with paper towels and have ready. Remove the outer leaves of the lettuce. Cut a V-shaped wedge around the inner core and remove the core and discard. Halve the lettuce to make 2 quarter sections. With a large, sharp knife, slice each section crosswise into a very, very thin julienne or julienne with a hand-held Japanese mandoline. Transfer the julienned lettuce to the paper towel–lined bowl to absorb any excess water exuded by the lettuce when sliced. Discard the paper towels, and in the same bowl, toss the lettuce with salsa and use immediately, or the lettuce will wilt.

½ head medium (6-inch diameter) iceberg lettuce

½ cup Salsa Fresca (page 130)

BAJA CABBAGE SLAW

MAKES 2 CUPS, ENOUGH FOR 8 TACOS ~ HEAT LEVEL 3
PREP TIME 10 MINUTES

This is the slaw that is served everywhere in Ensenada. It's the perfect accompaniment to the Baja style of fried fish taco, as it doesn't have much liquid to make the tempura batter–coated fish soggy. This slaw goes on the tortilla before the fish. Always look for small, bright green heads of cabbage. These have the smallest core and are sweeter, with a more subtle "cabbage-y" flavor. Avoid any that are pale to almost white, which are older and not as sweet.

★ ★ ★

Remove the outer leaves of the cabbage. Cut a V-shaped wedge around the tough inner core and remove the core and discard. Halve the cabbage to make 2 quarter sections. With a large, sharp knife, slice each section crosswise into a thin julienne (about ⅛ inch thick) or julienne with a hand-held Japanese mandoline. Transfer the julienned cabbage to a large bowl. In a bowl, mix together the mayonnaise, lime juice, and Tabasco. Toss the mayonnaise mixture with the cabbage, refrigerate, and use within a few hours.

½ head small (5-inch diameter) green cabbage

2 tablespoons regular mayonnaise (not light)

¾ teaspoon fresh lime juice

2 drops jalapeño Tabasco Sauce (optional)

PICKLED ONIONS WITH SWEET BELL PEPPERS

MAKES 4 CUPS ~ HEAT LEVEL 1 ~ PREP TIME 40 MINUTES

Although used with onions and bell peppers here, this pickling brine works wonderfully well for any type of vegetable you want *en escabeche*, a common preparation in Mexico. In late summer in New Mexico, as the days begin to shorten and nights get cooler, home cooks will often pickle the remaining abundance of their kitchen gardens to enjoy throughout the winter.

★ ★ ★

To prepare the pickling liquid, place the peppercorns, oregano, bay leaves, cloves, and garlic in cheesecloth and tie into a pouch. In a saucepan, place the seasoning bundle, the 2 cups water, vinegar, salt, and sugar and simmer over medium-low heat for 30 minutes. Remove and discard the seasoning pouch. Add the onions and bell peppers to the pickling liquid and bring to a boil over medium-high heat. Remove from the heat when the liquid comes to a boil. Transfer to a container.

The vegetables will keep in the liquid for about 1 month in the refrigerator.

8 whole black peppercorns

2 teaspoons dried Mexican oregano, toasted (page 161)

2 bay leaves

2 whole cloves

3 cloves garlic

2 cups water

2 cups distilled white vinegar

2½ teaspoons kosher salt

1½ tablespoons sugar

2 red onions, very thinly sliced

1 sweet red bell pepper, cored, seeded, and thinly sliced

1 sweet yellow bell pepper, cored, seeded, and thinly sliced

LICUADOS

These are the fresh fruit drinks of Mexico that you find at markets everywhere served from large ribbed glass jars. Vendors at Mexican markets will offer licuados of all flavors made from local fruit, sugar, and water in a kaleidoscope of colors—hot pinks and greens from melons, yellow from pineapple, purple from hibiscus blossoms, orange from tangerines. No two licuado stands are alike, and this drink represents, for me, the infinite variety and vitality of Mexican cuisine. If you go to Mexico, be sure to try the local licuado, since each region and locality has its own special tropical fruits and ingredients. I prefer to use cane sugar for licuados as it produces a noticeably brighter fruit flavor. For a more natural sugar, substitute a light agave syrup, using about one-fourth less than for cane sugar. If you have a juicer that both squeezes the fruit and strains the pulp, it will produce a fantastic licuado base with the purest fruit flavor. With really ripe, sweet fruit, decrease the amount of sugar in the recipe.

★ ★ ★

PINEAPPLE LICUADO

In the jar of a blender, add all the ingredients and pulse briefly until the pineapple chunks are finely chopped (but not a puree). You will have to add the ingredients in 2 batches. Strain through a medium-mesh strainer. Chill well in the refrigerator. Serve over ice with a garnish of fresh pineapple.

★ ★ ★

TANGERINE LICUADO

Combine all ingredients in a large bowl and whisk to blend. No need to strain. Chill well in the refrigerator. Serve over ice with a tangerine wheel for garnish.

PINEAPPLE LICUADO
MAKES 8 CUPS

2 cups pineapple juice (preferably unsweetened, from the refrigerator section of the market)

½ fresh pineapple, peeled, cored, and cut into large chunks, plus more chunks for garnish

5 cups cold water (preferably spring water)

5 tablespoons sugar

2 tablespoons freshly squeezed lime juice

TANGERINE LICUADO
MAKES 8 CUPS

3 cups tangerine juice (preferably unsweetened, from the refrigerator section of the market)

1 cup freshly squeezed tangerine, clementine, or orange juice

4 cups cold water (preferably spring water)

6 tablespoons sugar

INGREDIENTS AND TECHNIQUES

Become comfortable with the ingredients, equipment, and particularly the techniques described here, commonly used in Mexican and Southwestern cuisine. They are specific to the recipes in this book and are arranged in alphabetical order for easy reference. It is always best to use fresh ingredients, and none of the New World cuisines make a habit of using less than suitable foodstuffs. But also keep in mind that in the world of Mexican cooking, technique equals flavor—toasting and grinding whole spices and seeds so they are intensely aromatic, blistering tomatoes and chiles to draw out their richness and depth, roasting garlic until soft and sweet. Techniques like these, passed on for centuries, remain at the heart of this recipe collection and their rustically robust flavors.

★ ★ ★

ACHIOTE (ANNATTO) PASTE

Solid blocks of red paste that combine brick-red annatto seeds, citrus juices, chiles, and dried spices like black pepper, cumin, oregano, and allspice. The small annatto seeds are a signature of Mexico's Yucatán cuisine and the markets of that region. They have a distinctive, iodine-like flavor and a deep hue, giving earthiness to chicken, pork, and fish and infusing food with a brick-red color. Look for the paste in Hispanic markets, chain supermarkets located in Hispanic communities, and well-stocked specialty stores.

★ ★ ★

AVOCADO

This is the rich, silken, green-fleshed fruit of the Americas. I prefer the purplish-black, bumpy-skinned Haas avocado with its rich, buttery flesh to the smoother, green-skinned Fuerte, which is more watery. Buy avocados in advance of when you need them, as they are usually sold before they are ripe. To ripen at home, hold at room temperature for two to three days until the flesh just "breaks" (gives a little to the touch).

To pit: Halve first by slicing lengthwise (top to bottom) and twisting to separate. Then, lightly chop the pit with a chef's knife and give it a sideways twist; the avocado pit will release from its flesh. Knock the pit off the knife. If you mash a lot of avocado flesh but won't use it right away, reserve the pits and bury them in the mashed avocado, as they help prevent oxidation.

To slice or dice: Halve and pit the avocado, then slice or cube the flesh in the peel and scoop out with a spoon.

★ ★ ★

BEANS

There are a great many varieties of beans available, and they all are inexpensive, nutritious, and tasty. Beans are best cooked very slowly (just below a simmer) in a heavy, covered pot in a minimal amount of liquid so they finish meltingly tender and flavorful. Don't add salt until the end of cooking time or the beans will be tough.

In general, soaking beans before cooking them is not necessary, although some recipes will call for it. Soaking helps soften old beans or certain types of heirloom beans, but these days, beans tend to be quite fresh, and soaking only loosens the husks, which makes for messy beans. To head off gastric discomfort (gassiness) when eating beans, add the herb epazote (see *Epazote*) to the beans as they cook.

Black beans: Also called turtle beans, these are actually a very dark purple. They are native to Central and South America and are widely used in the Caribbean. With their strong, smoky flavor, they are my favorite beans.

Pinto beans: Native to the Southwest, and a variety of the common kidney bean, the pinto is the most popular bean in the United States and one of the most nutritious. Literally meaning "painted," the pinto is beige with brownish-pink streaks and turns a uniform pink when cooked. Slightly bland, they are a good base for high-flavor ingredients like bacon, onions, garlic, chiles, and spices.

* * *

BELL PEPPERS

Also known as sweet peppers, this chile pepper relative is not fiery hot, but rather sweet, crisp, and refreshing. Sweet peppers are not a substitute for chile peppers, but work well in combination with them. Colors range from red to yellow to green, purple, and orange. Green bell peppers are the most common, but their overpowering green, unripe, or "vegetable" flavor is not compatible with other Southwestern flavors. Roasting and peeling sweet peppers get rid of the tough skin and improve their flavor.

To core and seed: Slice off the top and bottom. Slit open the pepper and trim away the ribs and scrape off the seeds with a knife.

To julienne: Cut into thin strips (see *Julienne; Rajas*).

To dice: Cut into strips, then cut crosswise into cubes as specified in the recipe.

To oil-roast: In a heavy-bottomed pan, heat 2 inches of canola oil to 375°F. Carefully add 1 or 2 sweet peppers to the hot oil (roast just a few at a time so they don't crowd each other and lower the temperature of the oil). Turn them as the submerged part of the pepper begins to blister, 1½ minutes per side. Keep turning as necessary until all sides are blistered, but not burned.

To peel: Place the roasted pepper in a bowl, cover with a clean kitchen towel or plastic wrap, and let sit for 15 minutes (if stuffing the pepper, don't cover after roasting; it will get too soft and be harder to fill). Peel off the skin with your fingers or the tip of a knife; the flesh underneath should have darkened in color. **Do not rinse the peeled pepper or wipe it too much as the natural oils—and much of the flavor—will wash away.** Split open the pepper and remove the seeds and veins with a knife. There is no need to peel sweet peppers that you will puree and strain.

* * *

BLENDER

The most commonly used small appliance for Southwestern and Mexican cuisine, the blender is perfect for preparing chile sauces and some salsas. It is better than a food processor for small amounts, and purees ingredients to a finer consistency.

* * *

BUTANE TORCH

A small handheld kitchen torch is especially useful if you need a flame and your cooktop is electric rather than gas. You'll find it handy for blistering and blackening tomatoes, as well as caramelizing desserts. Well-stocked kitchenware stores sell them.

* * *

CACTUS (NOPALES; NOPALITOS)

The "leaves" or paddles of the pickly pear cactus are a common ingredient in the American Southwest and in central Mexico. A cross in taste between green beans and okra, they have a wonderful flavor when cooked, grilled, or used in salsas. Use them as a vegetable and cook them, covered, either very quickly when you want to preserve their bright, fresh color and crisp texture for salads and garnishes, or very slowly when they are part of soups and stews. If you are blanching them in water (for a salad, for example), add some tomatillo husks, which magically prevent the paddles from becoming slimy and losing their color. Before they are cooked, you must extract the very thin spines that cover the paddles: Protect your hands with work gloves and scrape away the spines with a vegetable peeler or paring knife. Proceed as directed in the recipe. You can buy fresh nopales at specialty produce markets, Hispanic markets, and chain supermarkets located in Hispanic neighborhoods, sometimes with spines already removed. Use them soon after purchasing as they soften quickly. Sliced or diced cactus is sold in cans or jars as nopalitos, packed in water or pickling brine. Rinse canned nopalitos before using.

★ ★ ★

CANELA

Mexican cinnamon—canela—is lighter in color, with a softer bark and a milder, sweeter flavor than the hard-stick cinnamon common in the United States—in fact, they are different varieties. Stick canela is soft enough to be ground in a *molcajete* or an electric spice grinder with relative ease. In Mexican and Southwestern cooking, canela is used in both sweet and savory dishes. Substitute about half the amount of regular ground cinnamon or stick cinnamon for ground or stick canela, if necessary. Canela is sold at some Hispanic markets and online (see Sources, page 167).

★ ★ ★

CHEESES, MEXICAN

Throughout Latin America, wonderful regional specialty cheeses prevail in markets. You can find Mexican cheeses at Hispanic markets, chain supermarkets located in Hispanic communities, or at the cheese counters of some specialty food stores.

Asadero: Made from cow's milk, semisoft asadero is buttery and slightly tangy, with a little more flavor than some of the other Mexican "melting" cheeses. One of the most popular uses is as a filling for quesadillas and tacos. If you can't find it, substitute Munster cheese.

Chihuahua: This mild, salty, slightly sour, semisoft-to-semihard cow's milk cheese is also called *queso menonito* after the original producers—Canadian Mennonites who settled in the Mexican state of Chihuahua in the 1920s (now both non-Mennonites and Mennonites make it). Common uses are for quesadillas, fillings, and part of the blend

for queso fundido. A young jack cheese is an acceptable substitute.

Queso fresco: Mexico's most popular fresh cheese is usually made from part-skim cow's milk (sometimes blended with goat's milk) and is moist, crumbly, mildly salty, and a bit sharp. It doesn't melt. Rather it's grated and used in salads, over refried beans and chile rajas, as part of a blend for quesadillas, or in stuffings for squash blossoms. Acceptable substitutes include a moist farmer's cheese, dry cottage cheese, or a mild feta cheese—all improved with a little cream and salt.

Queso Oaxaca: Good as a filling for quesadillas and rellenos and a very popular ingredient, this slightly tangy cow's milk cheese is sold in braids or balls and gets stringy when cooked. Fresh mozzarella cheese is similar, but milder. The cheese originated in Oaxaca, hence its name. Acceptable substitutes include Monterey jack, Munster, or a domestic Fontina.

★ ★ ★

CHILE CARIBE

A seasoning made from crushed dried red chiles, this is the familiar red pepper flakes offered as a condiment in every pizza restaurant. Having seeds and a coarse texture, chile caribe is best used as a base for chile sauces or other rustic dishes. Although older crushed chiles with a pale color are typically used for this seasoning, fresh chile caribe should have the vibrancy of dried red chile, freshly crushed. Available at Hispanic markets, specialty food stores, chain supermarkets (as red pepper flakes), or online (see Sources, page 167).

★ ★ ★

CHILE POWDERS

Pure chile powders are made exclusively from one type of chile—and nothing else. They are traditionally used to make chile sauces and as a seasoning for everything from tamales to pasta to breads. A good quality chile powder should have a deep, rich color and not be powdery or dry (a slightly lumpy consistency is a sign that the natural oils are still fresh). Avoid buying commercial chile powder mixes as they are not pure flavors. Rather they contain onion powder or garlic powder (or both), black pepper, salt, cumin, and paprika—and very little real chile powder, which is the essential ingredient. Store chile powder in the refrigerator or a cool, dark place up to 6 months. You will likely find the freshest (and cheapest) pure chile powders in Hispanic markets, usually labeled as mild, medium, or hot. If more than one brand is available, choose the chile powder with the deepest hue—a sign of quality. They are also available by mail order (see Sources, page 167). To grind your own, see *Chiles, Dried*.

★ ★ ★

CHILES, DRIED

Ounce for ounce, a dried chile packs a more potent punch than just about anything else in the kitchen larder. The drying process intensifies and magnifies the flavors of the chile much like a raisin is so much more intense than the seedless grape it starts out as. As a result, a dried chile tends to have a much more distinctive taste than its fresh counterpart, with flavors that are so much more complex and intense. When shopping for chiles, be aware that fresh and dried forms of the same chile can have different names. Buy dried chiles that are flexible (a sign of freshness), with uniform color. They should be dark and brilliant, with no white spots or other signs of deterioration, and have a pleasant aroma. Avoid any that are broken as the essential oils that give them flavor likely have evaporated. Store dried chiles airtight in a cool, dry place; they are at their best if used within 6 months.

In Southwestern cuisine, dried chiles are roasted, soaked to reconstitute, then pureed and usually used for sauces. In the Mexican kitchen, dried chiles are roasted until they are almost burned to develop an even more intense color and flavor. Unless your recipe suggests a different procedure, here are general instructions.

To dry-roast: Stem and seed the chiles. Heat a dry cast-iron or heavy-bottomed skillet or flat griddle over high heat, decrease the heat to medium-high, and dry-roast the chiles for 3 to 4 minutes. Or place the chiles on a baking sheet in a 250°F oven and dry-roast the same amount of time. Shake them once or twice and watch that they don't scorch and become bitter.

To rehydrate: Fill a pan about one-fourth the way up the sides with water and set on the stove. In a stainless steel bowl, place the dry-roasted chiles and just enough water to cover after pushing the chiles down (too much water will wash away the flavor). Rest the bowl on the pot of water and heat to just below boiling over medium heat, pressing the chiles down with the pot lid or a plate. Remove from the heat and let them soak until soft, 15 to 20 minutes. Use as directed in the recipe. (Some recipes may require that you reserve the soaking water to make a chile sauce; if the water is bitter, don't use it.) If you prefer, steam dried chiles over simmering water until soft and pliable, about 20 to 30 minutes.

To make pure chile powder: It's possible to grind dried chiles into a powder in a spice grinder, but it's a tedious process to produce the amounts needed for cooking. It's better to buy quality chile powders from a store or supplier with a large turnover so you know the spice is fresh.

Ají: The family of chiles from South America. The *ají panca*, the type used in this book, is a mild chile with berry flavors used in chile sauces and fish dishes. It is dark brown, wrinkled, and tapers to a point, measuring 3 to 5 inches long and 1 to 1½ inches across. Heat: 1–2

Ancho: A dried poblano chile and the most commonly used dried chile in Mexico, the ancho is brick red to dark mahogany, wrinkled, with broad shoulders (in Spanish, *ancho* means wide), and measures 5 inches long by 3 inches wide. The sweetest of the dried chiles, its flavor is both fruity and woodsy and is at its best when flexible and aromatic. It is frequently mislabeled as a pasilla. Heat: 3–5

Árbol: Literally "tree" chile and related to the cayenne, the *chile de árbol* is bright brick-red, skinny, and 2 to 3 inches long. It delivers a pungent, sweet flavor and searing heat. It's primarily used in powdered form for sauces and also in soups and stews. Heat: 7–8

Cascabel: A dark cherry color, smooth, and round, measuring about 1½ inches in diameter, the cascabel rattles when shaken (in Spanish, *cascabel* means rattle). The rich flavors are a little smoky and woodsy—wonderful in salsas, sauces, soups, and stews. Heat: 4

Chipotle: These are usually dried, smoked jalapeño chiles (there are eight different types of chipotles in Mexico) that are used mainly in soups, salsas, and sauces for their smoky-sweet flavor and subtle, yet deep heat. Measuring 2 to 4 inches long, they are crinkly and dark brown. Chipotle chiles en adobo are canned, dried smoked jalapeño chiles stewed with onions, tomatoes, vinegar, and spices. Heat: 5–6

Chipotle puree: Make this yourself to give a flavor boost to a variety of recipes: Puree a can of chipotles in adobo sauce in a blender and store airtight in the refrigerator for up to 1 month.

Guajillo: The shiny, deep orange-red *guajillo* (little gourd) combines sweet heat and earthy flavors. It's one of the most common cultivars grown in Mexico and measures about 4 inches long and 1½ inches wide. You can use this chile as a substitute for the New Mexico chile. Heat: 2–4

New Mexico (red): Also known as the *chile colorado* and the dried California chile, it is bright scarlet and about 6 inches long and 1½ inches across. With earthy flavors and crisp, clear heat, it is an indispensable ingredient in certain traditional red chile sauces. It appears everywhere in the form of crushed dried flakes and ground chile powders. Heat: 2–4

Pasilla: This dried *chilaca* chile is aptly name "little raisin." Also known as *chile negro*, it is wrinkled, almost black in color, and about 5 inches long and 1 inch wide. Poblanos, fresh and dried, are often mistakenly called pasillas. A key chile in traditional mole sauce, the pasilla is also wonderful in other sauces, especially for seafood. Heat: 3–5

Pasilla de Oaxaca: Shiny red-mahogany, very wrinkled, and measuring about 3 to 4 inches long and 1 to 1½ inches across, this smoked chipotle chile is grown only in the Oaxaca region of Mexico. It offers an acrid fruit-smoke flavor and a sharp, lingering heat. It is not related to the pasilla, but likely got its name because the colors are similar. Heat: 6–7

★ ★ ★

CHILES, FRESH

Most chiles are green while unripe and turn to shades of red, orange, yellow, or brown when mature. In cooking, many chiles are used both green and fully ripened. Often they are the same chile—the New Mexico green (unripe) and New Mexico red (ripe). Buy fresh chiles with bright, smooth, unbroken skins. They should be firm and unblemished, with a fresh, sharp aroma. Store them wrapped in paper towels (not in a plastic bag, which speeds spoilage) in the refrigerator for 2 to 3 weeks. When a recipe calls for fresh chiles and none are available locally, commercially frozen chiles are the next best thing. Hispanic markets, many chain supermarkets, and specialty produce stores offer a selection of fresh chiles. Fresh New Mexico green chiles, my favorite, are available in the Southwest and by mail order. Frozen chiles are available at Hispanic markets or online. See Sources, page 167.

Handle chiles with care—they get their fire from the potent chemical capsaicin in their ribs and seeds that can burn the skin and eyes. Wear disposable gloves when preparing chiles. Don't touch your face or eyes as you work, and wash hands thoroughly when you are done.

Fresh chiles are commonly roasted and peeled to deepen flavor and, if desired, help loosen the skin so it is easier to remove. Chiles blackened over a gas flame or under a broiler can sometimes pick up the flavor of the heat source, which is not always desirable. Unless your recipe suggests a different procedure, here are general instructions for two methods that work well.

To dry-roast: For smooth-skinned chiles like jalapeños and serranos, as well as fruits like tomatoes and tomatillos. Heat a dry cast-iron or heavy-bottomed skillet or flat griddle over medium heat. Place the chiles in the hot pan and cook, turning every 5 minutes, until all sides are evenly blistered. The skin can char a bit, but the goal is to loosen the skin, but keep it intact, and cook the flesh partially without it breaking down and becoming too soft.

To oil-roast: Use this method for chiles that you want to stuff, for a clean, sweet vegetable flavor without smoke, for a sauce or recipe that requires chiles with a deep green color, or for chiles whose ridges and valleys (like poblanos and sweet peppers) would blister unevenly with other roasting methods. In a heavy-bottomed pan, heat 2 inches of canola oil to 375°F. Carefully add 1 or 2 whole chiles to the hot oil (roast just a few at a time so they don't crowd each other and lower the temperature of the oil). Turn them as the submerged part of the chiles begins to blister, 1½ minutes per side. Turn the chiles as necessary until all sides are blistered, but not burned. **Do not wash the chiles after roasting or you'll lose flavor.**

To peel: Place the roasted chile in a bowl, cover with a clean kitchen towel or plastic wrap, and let sit for 15 minutes (if stuffing the chile, don't cover after roasting; it will get soft and be harder to fill). Peel off the skin with your fingers or scrape off with the dull edge of a knife; the flesh underneath should have darkened in color. Do not rinse the peeled chile as the natural oils—and much of the roasted flavor—will wash away. Split open the chiles and if desired, remove the seeds and veins with a knife.

Anaheim: The mildest of the fresh green chiles, the Anaheim is also known as the California or long green chile. It is bright green (red, when ripe), tapered and about 6 inches long and 2 inches around, and excellent stuffed or in chile stews. In most cases, substitute the Anaheim (mixed with roasted jalapeños) if the recipe calls for the New Mexico green and it isn't available. Anaheims are available all year long in almost all grocery stores and supermarkets in the United States. Heat: 2–3

Fresno (red): This jalapeño lookalike (they are different varieties) is a wax-type chile, thick-fleshed, sweet, and hot. Also known as *chile caribe*, it tapers to a rounded end and measures about 2 inches long and 1 inch in diameter. It's excellent in salsas, ceviches, stuffings, breads, sauces, and pickled (en escabeche). Heat: 6–7

Güero: A generic name for yellow chiles (from the Spanish, for light-skinned or blond) that usually applies to pale yellow tapered chiles such as the Hungarian wax or banana chiles, or the Santa Fe grande. Varies in size from 3 to 5 inches long, and in strength from medium to hot. It's primarily used for yellow mole sauces, but also in other sauces, in salads, or pickled (en escabeche). Heat: 4–7

Habanero: The habanero ("from Havana") is small—2 inches long and about 1½ inches across—and the hottest of all chiles available in the United States and Mexico (there are hotter chiles grown in India). Colors range from dark green to orange, orange-red, or red when fully ripe. Users beware! It has a fierce, intense heat that demands respect and careful handling (wear gloves). But its distinctive fruity flavor really wakes up a timid dish, or any salsa, sauce, marinade, or condiment. Heat: 10

Jalapeño: To Americans, this green chile is probably the most familiar of all hot chiles. It benefits anything that needs a little heat: salsas, stews, breads, sauces, dips, and more. Small, tapered, and rounded, it measures about 2 inches long and 1 inch wide. Pickled jalapeños are available in brine packed in cans and jars. When dried and smoked, the sweeter red jalapeño chile is sold as a chipotle. Heat: 5–6

New Mexico (green): This is the basic chile in New Mexican cuisine. Also known as the long green chile, it

measures 6 to 9 inches long and about 1½ inches across. It tapers like the Anaheim, but its flavor is hotter, clearer, and more intense—and unlike any other chile in North America. It is available fresh almost all year, but most of the fresh crop is roasted locally in the fall. The fresh chiles freeze well, and frozen chiles are better than canned. In most cases, substitute the Anaheim (mixed with roasted jalapeños) if the recipe calls for the New Mexico green and it isn't available. Heat: 3–5

Poblano: So dark green it almost looks purple-black, the pointy poblano is often mislabeled a pasilla (a dried chile, and altogether different). It's the chile ancestor to the sweet bell pepper, which shares a similar shape. It measure about 4 inches long and 2½ inches wide. It is always roasted for a fuller, smoky, earthy flavor, and is big and thick-walled enough to stuff. Also good as rajas (strips) or in sauces. Heat: 3

Serrano: The hottest of the fresh green chiles that are most commonly available in Hispanic markets and supermarkets in the United States, the serrano is bright dark green to scarlet, cylindrical, and skinny—about 2 inches long and ½ inch wide. Both colors are interchangeable in cooking, with the red a little sweeter. It's excellent in salsas, pickled (en escabeche), or roasted and used in sauces. Heat: 7

★ ★ ★

CHORIZO

Mexican chorizo is a fresh spicy mixture of coarsely chopped pork and seasonings like garlic, spices, and chile powder, typically sold in bulk or in links. If in links, remove the casing before using. Bulk chorizo is ready to use as is. Spanish chorizo is cured and more firm. During cooking, the chorizo should stay soft, not get hard like dry bacon (if necessary, add a little water to the pan to keep the meat soft) and make use of all the flavored oil that renders out during cooking. The fat gives eggs cooked with chorizo delicious flavor and tender texture. Chorizo is available at Hispanic markets and most chain supermarkets.

★ ★ ★

CILANTRO

Mexican and Southwestern restaurants buy this pungent sweet herb by the case, it's so prevalent a flavor in those cuisines. Buy fresh green bunches that look crisp and unwilted. The leaves are edible and best when young; discard the stems and any yellow or discolored leaves. For the recipes in this book, we use only the leaves. The plant's seeds (sold as coriander seed) are dried and used as a spice.

★ ★ ★

CLARIFIED BUTTER

The golden liquid left when unsalted butter is slowly melted until the milk solids separate out (and are discarded) and any top froth skimmed off. It can withstand high heat because of its higher smoking temperature, which is why it is often used for sautéing (it will still burn, though, at very high heat). To keep it below the burning point but retain the butter flavor, sauté with a mixture of 1 tablespoon vegetable oil to 1 cup clarified butter.

★ ★ ★

COMAL

The all-purpose Mexican cookware in the form of a large, flat cooking surface that is set over a stove burner or on a grate over a wood fire. A comal is traditionally made of thin unglazed clay that is slightly porous so it absorbs moisture for better browning, but versions made of cast-iron or black steel are also available. In Mexico, they are made out of clay and treated with a lime mineral slip. It works particularly well for cooking and rewarming tortillas and toasting herbs, spices, and seeds. A cast-iron or heavy-bottomed skillet that holds and distributes heat well can substitute.

* * *

CORN

Besides rice and wheat, corn is one of the great staple foods of the earth, and *the* staple food of the Americas. A sacred plant in the Southwest, corn has been cultivated by the Hopis for two thousand years, and further south, in Mexico, for at least three thousand years before that. With an infinite variety of shapes and colors (there are over eight thousand varieties), corn remains an important and ever-present ingredient in both Southwestern and Mexican cuisines. Roasting corn deepens its flavor and infuses an appealing smokiness.

To dry-roast: Cut off the kernels from ears of fresh corn with a sharp knife, avoiding the tough cob; check that the kernels are dry (not too much of the corn juices are included). Heat a large, heavy-bottomed dry nonstick skillet over high heat until almost smoking. Add 1 layer of corn kernels at a time, as you want all the kernels to come into contact with the hot pan surface, or the corn will steam, not roast. Dry-roast, tossing constantly, until the kernels are smoky and caramelized, but still moist, 4 to 5 minutes.

* * *

CUMIN

Spanish conquistadors brought cumin to the Americas, where it quickly took root in native cuisines (the Moors introduced cumin to the Spanish after bringing it to Spain from India). Cumin is an earthy, pervasive spice that complements dried chiles and roasted foods. The flavor of toasted and ground cumin seed is better than that of cumin powder (see *Grinding Seeds and Spices; Toasting Seeds, Spices, and Herbs*).

* * *

DEEP-FRYING

The best cookware for home frying is a large, tall, stable, heavy-bottomed pot, used together with a deep-fat thermometer, which allows precise control of cooking and browning. For these recipes, fry with a neutral vegetable oil like canola oil and never fill the pot more than half full. The key to successful frying is to maintain temperature so the food gets crisp and golden, but not burned, and to not overcrowd the pot, which can cause the temperature to drop and the food to be greasy. Fry in batches, if necessary, and be sure the oil returns to temperature before adding more food. After each use, filter the oil through cheesecloth or a fine strainer, which keeps it fresher longer for reuse, although oil picks up the flavors of what it fries. If the oil is strained after each use, you can reuse it two or three times if frying the same type of ingredient—vegetables, for example.

* * *

DICE

To cut food into small, even cubes. Small dice: ⅛-inch cubes. Medium dice: ¼-inch cubes. Large dice: ½-inch cubes. To dice, cut food into ⅛, ¼, or ½-inch-thick slices (or the size the recipe calls for). Stack the slices and cut matchsticks of the same thickness. Then cut the sticks crosswise into cubes.

* * *

DRY-ROASTING

See *Corn; Chiles, Dried; Chiles, Fresh; Garlic; Tomatoes; Tomatillos.*

★ ★ ★

EPAZOTE

Also known as wormseed or skunkweed, epazote is a pungent herb with an offputting aroma and flavor that both grow on you. It's primarily used in Mexican and Southwestern cooking. Added to beans as they cook, it helps reduce gastric discomfort (gassiness) when the beans are eaten. Look for epazote at most Hispanic markets in fresh and dried form. It's also very easy to grow in pots.

★ ★ ★

ESCABECHE

Foods preserved in brine, usually a mixture of vinegar, chiles, and spices, are called *en escabeche* (pickled). This technique is most commonly used for vegetables, but also for meat, fish, and eggs.

Escabeche vegetables for turkey: In a nonreactive container, combine 2 teaspoons freshly ground black pepper, 1 teaspoon kosher salt, 2½ teaspoons toasted and ground dried Mexican oregano (page 161), 3 stemmed and thinly sliced güero chiles, 4 stemmed and thinly sliced Fresno chiles, 1 thinly sliced white onion, 3 bay leaves, 2 sticks of canela, 1 tablespoon toasted and ground coriander seed (page 164), 1 medium sweet red bell pepper (cored, seeded, and cut into very thin strips), 3 ounces drained pickled jalapeño slices, ½ cup liquid from the can of pickled jalapeños, ½ teaspoon toasted and ground fennel seed, ¼ teaspoon ground allspice, 2 tablespoons sugar, 1 cup unseasoned rice wine vinegar, 1 cup water, 1 tablespoon olive oil, 1 small julienned carrot, ½ cup very thinly sliced fennel, and 2 tablespoons lemon-infused olive oil (page 162). Refrigerate until ready to use in Escabeche Turkey with Pickled Vegetables (page 50).

★ ★ ★

FOOD PROCESSOR

A handy tool in the modern kitchen, the food processor can replace much of the work formerly done by mortar and pestle. It's excellent for coarse-textured sauces. But it tends to mash foods rather than cut them, so delicate salsas are still best prepared by hand and purees rendered more silken by a blender.

★ ★ ★

GARLIC

Roasted to draw out its sweetness and mellow its bite, garlic is a foundation of Southwestern cuisine. Buy whole heads of very fresh garlic and snap off and peel individual cloves as you need them. Avoid prepeeled garlic, as the cloves are peeled by machine, which can bruise the garlic, exposing it to oxygen, which makes it taste stronger.

To peel: Lay cloves on a work surface and hit with the side of a chef's knife or bottom of a skillet. The thin skin will pull off.

To mince: Peel the cloves. Slice thinly, cut crosswise into tiny pieces, and chop as finely as needed.

To dry-roast: In a dry cast-iron or heavy-bottomed skillet, place unpeeled garlic cloves and dry-roast over low heat until the garlic softens, 30 to 40 minutes. Shake the pan occasionally. Or, roast garlic cloves in a preheated 350°F oven until soft, 20 to 30 minutes. When done, the garlic should be creamy and sweet, and soft enough to slip out of the skin when you squeeze the clove.

★ ★ ★

GRINDING SEEDS AND SPICES

Ground just when you need them, whole spices are fresh and intensely flavorful. Use a small electric spice mill (or a coffee grinder), preferably reserved for this purpose, or by hand with a mortar and pestle. If the machine must do double duty for spices and coffee, wash the container thoroughly after each use. Grinding kosher salt or dry rice after each use will remove spice odors.

* * *

HOJA SANTA

Commonly used in Mexican cooking, hoja santa (also known as *yerba santa* and holy leaf) has heart-shaped leaves and a wonderful taste like sassafras or root beer. Fresh or dried tarragon can be substituted (use 2 tablespoons fresh tarragon or 1 tablespoon dried). If you buy it in bulk, blanch the leaves for a second to preserve color, then puree with a little water and freeze in cubes to use in pipiáns, soups, sauces, and moles.

* * *

HUITLACOCHE

A prized delicacy in Mexico, this delicious, exotic-looking, grayish fungus grows on corn and tastes like wild morels. Its earthy, robust flavor gave rise to its nickname—Mexican (or New World) truffle. In Mexico, the fresh fungus is sold in markets and is very costly. It is available frozen and canned at well-stocked Hispanic markets or online (see Sources, page 167).

* * *

JULIENNE

Thin, even strips of foods like carrots or potatoes, usually 2 to 3 inches long and ¼ inch wide, and the technique of making them. To julienne, cut the food into ¼-inch (or the size the recipe calls for) slices, stack the slices, and cut into ¼-inch (or other size) matchsticks. Cut crosswise, if necessary, to create strips of the desired length.

* * *

JUNIPER BERRIES

Like sage, juniper brings to mind the aromas of the open range of the American Southwest, where they both flourish. The berries are blue-gray with an aromatic woodsy fragrance and are available dried in most supermarket spice sections.

* * *

LARD

Mexican lard is made by slowly rendering fresh pork fat. Rich and flavorful, it makes a good fat for frying or refrying Southwestern foods and produces very tender, flaky pastries. You can easily make your own lard at home by gently simmering finely chopped fat with water 4 to 5 hours, uncovered, adding spices, if you want, to create more interesting flavors. In comparison, commercial lard, the type sold at most supermarkets, is hydrogenated and stabilized, with an unappealing flavor. Fresh lard keeps for several months in the refrigerator. Most supermarkets carry lard in some form. Look for fresh, refrigerated Mexican lard at Hispanic markets and butcher shops and chain supermarkets located in Hispanic communities.

* * *

LIME JUICER

Very efficient, this hinged, molded plastic or cast-aluminum tool, often with a lime-green powder coating, effectively squeezes out the juice from a fresh lime. By inverting a lime half, it presses out the flavorful juice even better than a hand-held wooden reamer, trapping the rind, pulp, and seeds. The larger size handles lemons, but works for limes, too.

* * *

MANGOES

The most widely consumed fruit in the world and available in many varieties. Mangoes are oval or round, with a large, flat seed, golden flesh that is delectably sweet and juicy, and yellow-orange skin with a rosy blush. Choose fruit that is ripe, fragrant, and slightly soft to the touch for eating, and slightly underripe for salsas. A little lime juice draws out their full tropical flavor and richness.

To peel and seed: Stand it on its wide end, narrow side toward you. With a sharp knife, cut down along the seed on both sides to cut away the fruit; discard the seed. Scoop out the fruit from both pieces and discard the peel.

To dice: Cut away the flesh from both sides of the seed. With a sharp, pointed knife, score the flesh into squares down to, but not through, the skin. Invert the skin to pop up the squares, and slice them off.

* * *

MASA

The dough primarily used to make tortillas and the edible casing for tamale fillings. Masa is made from dried corn kernels that have been soaked, then steeped in an alkaline solution of water and slaked lime (cal) to soften the kernels and loosen the hard outer hull. The limed kernels—*nixtamal* in Spanish—are then rinsed and ground by machine or by stone grinding into apaste, the basis for masa. Stone-ground masa preserves more of the nutritional benefits and flavor as metal grinders heat up during the milling process from friction, which in turns heats the masa and slightly "cooks" it. Fresh masa is carried at most Mexican markets or tortilla shops (*tortillerias*); ask for masa simple for tortillas, not masa for tamales, as the texture of the latter won't work for tortillas.

* * *

MASA HARINA

A flour of dehydrated masa (the dough made from treated dried corn). To reconstitute for making corn tortillas, masa harina is mixed with water and beaten to form a dough (although some chefs say that tortillas made with masa harina are not as supple as those made with fresh masa). Not cornmeal and sometimes labeled "corn flour," masa harina is readily available at most chain supermarkets through the United States, with Maseca and Quaker Oats the most common brands. Masa harina can quickly turn rancid, so be sure to buy from a store with a high turnover. Taste it before you use it, and once the package is opened, use within 1 month. See *Masa*.

* * *

MEXICAN CHOCOLATE

Not a pure chocolate, this a chocolate blend that typically includes cacao, cinnamon, sugar, and often ground almonds, which makes the best hot chocolate in the world! Most well-stocked supermarkets and Hispanic markets carry Ibarra or other brands of Mexican chocolate, packed as individual hard cakes in colorful yellow boxes.

* * *

MEXICAN CREMA

The Mexican equivalent of crème fraîche, crema is often served with Southwestern dishes as a relief to spicy food, as well as to provide richness—with refried beans or a spicy stew, for example. Crème fraîche and natural sour cream are acceptable substitutes.

To make Mexican-style crema, stir 2 tablespoons of buttermilk (preferably unpasteurized) into 1 cup of heavy cream, cover, and let sit out at warm room temperature (about 75°F) overnight to thicken. This homemade version will keep for up to 1 week in the refrigerator.

* * *

MEXICAN OREGANO

For Mexican and Southwestern cooking, pungent, weedy dried Mexican oregano is preferred over its more common Mediterranean counterpart, found on spice shelves in American supermarkets. It's a different variety and more potent, better able to stand up to spicy dishes. Hispanic markets usually stock it. Buy as dried leaves, not ground. To grind dried oregano, rub between your palms (a spice mill would grind it too fine). Dried oregano is often toasted before using. If substituting regular dried oregano leaves, use a little more. See *Toasting Seeds, Spices, and Herbs.*

* * *

MOLCAJETE Y TEJOLETE

The three-legged bowl and stubby pounder used as a grinding tool throughout the Americas for preparing salsas (giving them a superior silken texture and smoother blend of flavors) and guacamole, and for crushing herbs and spices. The traditional type carved of lava or basalt is highly recommended and can do double duty as a rustic serving bowl for salsas at buffet or party tables. Sets made of ribbed, unglazed earthenware and marble are also common. Find them in Hispanic markets, some well-stocked kitchenware stores, or by mail order. See *Mortar and Pestle.*

* * *

MOLE

The word *mole* is misunderstood. It comes from Nahuatl, the pre-Columbian language of Mexico, and means a sauce that is blended with more than one chile or more than one ingredient. Most Americans understand it to be the classic dark sauce of southern Mexico near Oaxaca and Peubla that contains many ingredients, including nuts, chiles, and chocolate. But there are also red moles, yellow moles,

as well as green moles that use only fresh chiles and fresh herbs.

* * *

MORTAR AND PESTLE

Simple, basic grinding tools comprised of a container (mortar) and pounder (pestle) used to grind herbs and spices and to mash ingredients to a paste. The interior of the mortar and end of the pestle should be rough in some way to better break down ingredients. Many cooks think the flavors of pastes and salsas are maximized when prepared slowly with a mortar and pestle, and superior to any produced by a machine. Particularly recommended are the Mexican *molcajete* and Japanese *suribachi.* See *Molcajete y Tejolete.*

* * *

MUSHROOMS

To sauté fresh mushrooms to a rich, golden color, use a pan large enough so they cook in one layer, which allows full contact with the hot cooking surface. If the pan is crowded, the pieces will steam and lack depth of flavor. I like to sauté fresh minced garlic with mushrooms; they pair well, and garlic gives the mushroom extra depth. To rehydrate dried mushrooms, soak them in a minimum amount of warm water until softened, 20 to 30 minutes. Drain and swirl briefly in fresh, warm water to remove any residual grit. Strain the soaking liquid through cheesecloth or paper coffee filter, if desired, and use in sauces, soups, or stews for woodsy flavor.

Porcini Paste: Rehydrate 1 ounce of dried porcini mushrooms in 1 cup warm water for about 30 minutes. Strain through a mesh sieve, reserving the mushrooms and soaking water separately. In a skillet over medium-high heat, add the reserved soaking water, 1 tablespoon olive oil, and ½ teaspoon minced garlic. Boil to reduce the liquid to a glaze, about 1 minute. Decrease the heat to very low, add the reserved mushrooms, ½ teaspoon kosher salt, and a pinch of black pepper, and cook about 10 minutes. Stir in 1 teaspoon white balsamic vinegar and remove from the heat. In the workbowl of a small food processor, add the mushroom mixture and puree to a smooth paste, or finely chop to a paste by hand. Makes about ½ cup paste. Store in the refrigerator.

★ ★ ★

NOPALES
See *Cactus.*

★ ★ ★

OLIVE OIL
In modern Southwestern and Mexican cooking, olive oil is sometimes used as a healthier oil alternative or to impart its distinctive flavor to a particular recipe. For these cuisines, I prefer the richer, more buttery Spanish extra-virgin olive oils, as their flavor is not as grassy and dominant as Italian Tuscans, and is the type used in the Americas since the arrival of Spanish missionaries and explorers.

Lemon-infused olive oil: Combine 1 cup good-quality Spanish extra-virgin olive oil with 4 teaspoons natural lemon flavor (I like Simply Organic brand), found in the spice sections of natural foods stores, well-stocked supermarkets, or specialty markets. Makes about 1 cup. Store at room temperature for 2 to 3 weeks.

★ ★ ★

ONIONS
Throughout Mexico, cooks prefer white onions over yellow as they are less sweet when cooked and have a bright, fresh onion flavor that isn't overwhelming. *Cebollitas,* grilled whole young green onions with small, bulbous white bases and tossed with salt and lime, is a popular taco garnish.

★ ★ ★

PAPAYAS
Juicy and exotic, pear-shaped papayas have smooth skin and luscious flesh that ranges in color from golden to deep salmon. Their small black seeds are usually discarded. Buy papayas when slightly underripe, with a yellow skin tinged with green like bananas. Let them ripen at room temperature until a uniform golden yellow and use quickly. As with mangoes, a squeeze of fresh lime juice plays up their tropical appeal.

★ ★ ★

PINE NUTS
Also known as *piñones,* pine nuts grow on the low, bushy *piñon* trees that dot the Southwestern landscape, especially in northern New Mexico. They are harvested in late fall, often as a family activity, by shaking the *piñon* trees so that kernels rain down out of the pine cones onto sheets spread below. The kernels are then split open, yielding the pine nuts. Pine nuts are rich, with a resiny taste that goes well with wild Southwestern flavors. Toasting deepens their flavor. See *Toasting Seeds, Spices, and Herbs.*

★ ★ ★

PUMPKIN SEEDS (PEPITAS)
In Mexican and Southwestern cooking, pumpkin seeds are used as an ingredient in chile sauces, pipiáns (sauces made with ground nuts or seeds), and moles, and are rich in protein. Pumpkin seeds lack the richness of pine nuts, but rather taste more like the vegetable itself. Raw (and sometimes toasted) pumpkin seeds are available at most natural foods stores. Try to buy them in bulk at a store with a high product turnover as they can quickly get rancid. For best nutrition and flavor, look for ones that have been sprouted and dried. Pumpkin seeds should be toasted for cooking; use a dry skillet and

toast lightly, just until they "pop." Don't let them get too dark. See *Toasting Seeds, Spices, and Herbs*.

* * *

RAJAS
"Slivers" or "strips," in Spanish. In Mexico and the Southwest it refers to julienned strips of roasted, peeled, and seeded chiles or sweet peppers. Typical size is about 3 inches long by ⅜ inch wide to use in soups, as a garnish, or with quesadillas, tacos, and tamales.

* * *

REFRY
A technique that adds flavor and texture to cooked foods such as beans or sauces. The ingredients are pureed or mashed and fried in fat, usually with fresh herbs for extra flavor. Refrying gives beans a crustier consistency and both marries and smooths out the flavors of chile sauces and makes them more complex. Typically, the puree is first passed through a medium-mesh strainer, quickly cooked in a tiny amount of hot oil in a very hot skillet (almost smoking), stirred to blend, and removed from the heat.

* * *

REHYDRATING CHILES
See *Chiles, Dried*.

* * *

SALT
Most recipes in this book call for coarse-grained kosher salt, additive-free and about half as salty as table salt. I prefer it because its larger grains distribute more easily in a mixture. Occasionally, when a salt with a light, fresh flavor is best, particularly with seafood, the choice is sea salt (produced by evaporation of sea water), as it is closest to the mineral content of the sea and, correspondingly, to the salt in the flesh of the seafood. I always undersalt, and build up to the natural level of the taste of the sea.

Smoked salt: Salt infused with wood smoke, which imparts the authentic aroma of cooking over an open fire or on a comal and adds that smoky element typical of Mexican food.

* * *

SQUASH BLOSSOMS
These deep yellow flowers of the squash plant, between 4 and 6 inches long, are commonly used dipped in batter and deep-fried, stuffed with goat cheese, sautéed as a vegetable, added to soups, or as a garnish. They are seasonally available, spring through fall, primarily at farmer's markets and specialty produce markets. Use within a day of purchase (store in the refrigerator), as they are delicate and very perishable.

* * *

TACO FRY BASKET
A convenient tool for for preparing multiple crispy taco shells at a time, this wire basket has slots (anywhere from 4 to 8) that shape corn tortillas into a U and hold them while they deep-fry in hot oil until crisp. They're sold through restaurant supply stores, well-stocked kitchenware shops, and online.

* * *

TACO HOLDER
For serving, this ceramic accessory has slots that hold filled crispy taco shells upright. Look for them at well-stocked kitchenware shops and online.

* * *

TAMARIND PASTE

The tart, yet sweet flavor of tamarind paste naturally complements many foods, including chiles. It's made from the hard seeds and bittersweet pulp of tamarind pods, the fruit of an evergreen tree from Asia and Mexico, which are boiled down into a paste. Look for the paste at Asian and Hispanic markets and well-stocked specialty food stores.

* * *

TOASTING SEEDS, SPICES, AND HERBS

Toasting gives herbs and spices a more intense flavor. To toast whole spices and seeds, place them in a hot, dry skillet over medium-high heat and toast, stirring frequently, until fragrant and a full shade darker, 2 to 3 minutes. Pumpkin seeds will take a little longer, 4 to 5 minutes, and pop when they are done.

To toast dried herbs, place them in a dry skillet over low heat and toast, stirring frequently, until fragrant and a slightly darker color, about 1 minute.

* * *

TOMATILLOS

Not a tomato, but a plum-sized, bright green fruit with a light brown husk that belongs to the Cape gooseberry family. Its bright sharp flavor, akin to rhubarb or green plums, makes it a favorite for salsas, sauces, and soups. Tomatillos are available fresh and canned at Hispanic markets and specialty produce stores. Select firm fresh tomatillos, with clean, straw-colored husks. Before using, remove the papery husk and rinse the fruit well, as its surface is sticky. (Save the husks for blanching nopales— cactus paddles, an old Mexican kitchen trick. Added to the blanching liquid, it prevents the nopales from becoming slimy and discolored.) Roasting (blackening)

tomatillos in their husks (removed after roasting) deepens their flavor.

To blacken: Keep the tomatillos whole with husk intact if dry-roasting. Dry-roast the tomatillos in a single layer in a dry cast-iron or wide, heavy-bottomed skillet over medium-high heat or on a baking sheet under a broiler (remove the husks first) until charred and blistered on all sides, about 20 minutes in a skillet or 5 minutes under a broiler. Remove the husk before using in a recipe.

* * *

TOMATOES

Among the many varieties, sizes, and shapes of tomatoes (which are indigenous to the Americas), it is the small, thick-walled Roma that is favored in the Mexican kitchen. Throughout Latin America, tomatoes are typically blackened to give them a more rustic, robust, and complex flavor—replicating the smoky depth of tomatoes roasted over an open wood fire or on a grill. I prefer the pear-shaped Roma tomato for its thicker pulp, less juice, and affinity for Southwestern ingredients. Small tomatoes work best for blackening, as the higher ratio of skin to flesh means more surface can be blackened, producing a smokier tomato flavor.

To blacken: Remove the stem of the tomato, but otherwise keep the tomato whole. Blacken the tomatoes in a single layer in a dry cast-iron or wide, heavy-bottomed skillet over medium-high heat or on a baking sheet under a broiler until charred and blistered on all sides, about 20 minutes in a skillet or 5 minutes under a broiler. You can blacken tomatoes with a butane kitchen torch, but it must be held very close (less than an inch) to the tomato to be effective.

* * *

TORTILLA PRESS

A hinged, two-piece device used to flatten masa (cornmeal dough) into thin flat disks for tortillas; some cooks also

use it to make a thin layer of masa for tamales. The tinned presses you see in Mexican markets are often porous castings that will easily break. The best, most durable ones are made of cast-iron or cast-aluminum, and also wood.

★ ★ ★

VEGETABLE OIL

For Mexican cooking, and the recipes in this book specifically, I generally use a neutral-flavored vegetable oil, meaning one that lacks a distinctive flavor. Healthy oils are canola, which has a fairly high smoke point, corn oil (a lower smoke point), or grapeseed oil (a very high smoke point). Look for pure, cold-pressed oils; Hain is a good brand.

★ ★ ★

VINEGAR

The bright acidity of vinegar is the high note in Mexican and Southwestern dishes like marinades, salsas, sauces, and grilled foods. In Mexico, mild fruit vinegars like ones made from overripe pineapples are commonly used. Unless otherwise specified, I prefer unflavored vinegars with lower acidity, like unseasoned rice wine vinegar or white balsamic vinegar.

SOURCES

BACON

The Grateful Palate
Tel. 888-472-5283
www.thegratefulpalate.com

★ ★ ★
BISON PRODUCERS

North American Bison Cooperative
Tel. 701-947-2505
www.nabison.com

★ ★ ★
BUFFALO AND ELK

Jackson Hole Buffalo Meat Co.
Tel. 307-732-6631
www.jhbuffalomeat.com

Jamison Farms
Tel. 800–ELK MEAT (800-355-6328)
www.jamisonfarms.com

Whole Foods Markets
www.wholefoodsmarkets.com

★ ★ ★
CHILE PLANTS

Cross Country Nurseries
Tel. 908-996-4646
www.chileplants.com

★ ★ ★
DRIED CHILES AND PURE CHILE POWDERS

Los Chileros
Tel. 888-EAT-CHILE (888-328-2445)
www.loschileros.com

★ ★ ★
HUITLACOCHE

Gourmet Sleuth
Tel. 408-354-8281
www.gourmetsleuth.com

★ ★ ★
MEXICAN INGREDIENTS, KITCHENWARE, AND SUPPLIES

La Tienda
Tel. 800-710-4304
www.latienda.com

Melissa Guerra
Tel. 877-875-2665
www.melissaguerra.com

Seasons of My Heart
Tel. (from United States and Canada)
011-52-1-951-508-0469
www.seasonsofmyheart.com

★ ★ ★

NEW MEXICO CHILES: FRESH, FROZEN, DRIED, SAUCES

Bueno Foods
Tel. 800-95-CHILE (800-952-4453)
www.buenofoods.com

Hatch Chile Express
Tel. 800-292-4454
www.hatch-chile.com

New Mexico Catalog
Tel. 888-678-0585
www.new-mexico-catalog.com

New Mexico Chili
Tel. 888-336-4228
www.nmchili.com

★ ★ ★

PECANS

Del Valle Pecans
Tel. 505-524-1867

★ ★ ★

SALT

Salt Traders
Tel. 800-641-SALT (800-641-7258)
www.salttraders.com

Salt Works
Tel. 425-885-7258
www.seasalt.com

★ ★ ★

SAUSAGE AND JERKY SUPPLIES, SMALL SMOKERS, RECIPES

The Sausage Maker Inc.
Tel. 888-490-8525
www.sausagemaker.com

★ ★ ★

SPANISH OLIVE OIL AND SPANISH PRODUCTS

The Spanish Table
Tel. 505-986-0243
www.tablespan.com

★ ★ ★

WILD GAME

Prairie Harvest
Tel. 800-350-7166
www.prairieharvest.com

★ ★ ★

WILD MUSHROOMS

FungusAmongUs
Tel. 360-568-3403
www.fungusamongus.com

Mycological Natural Products
Tel. 888-465-3247
www.mycological.com

INDEX

For James and Kelly, good friends and fellow taco trail travelers,
who helped me with this book and ate many, many tacos. And for
all the taco lovers out there.

All rights reserved. Published in the United States by Ten Speed Press, an imprint
of the Crown Publishing Group, a division of Random House, Inc., New York.
www.crownpublishing.com
www.tenspeed.com

Ten Speed Press and the Ten Speed Press colophon are registered trademarks
of Random House, Inc.

Library of Congress Cataloging-in-Publication Data on file with publisher

ISBN 978-1-58008-977-7

Printed in China

Cover and text design by Ed Anderson
Layout and production by BookMatters
Food and prop styling by Jenny Martin-Wong

11 10 9 8 7 6 5 4 3 2

First Edition